SADLIER'S
Coming to Faith Program

W9-BGN-360

COMING TO
GOD'S LOVE

Dr. Gerard F. Baumbach

Dr. Eleanor Ann Brownell

Moya Gullage

Helen Hemmer, I. H. M.

Gloria Hutchinson

Dr. Norman F. Josaitis

Rev. Michael J. Lanning, O. F. M.

Dr. Marie Murphy

Karen Ryan

Joseph F. Sweeney

The Ad Hoc Committee
to Oversee the Use of the Catechism,
National Conference of Catholic Bishops,
has found this catechetical text to be
in conformity with the
Catechism of the Catholic Church.

with

Dr. Thomas H. Groome
Boston College

Official Theological Consultant
    The Most Rev. Edward K. Braxton, Ph. D., S. T. D.

Scriptural Consultant
    Rev. Donald Senior, C. P., Ph. D., S. T. D.

Catechetical and Liturgical Consultants
    Dr. Gerard F. Baumbach
    Dr. Eleanor Ann Brownell

Pastoral Consultants
    Rev. Msgr. John F. Barry
    Rev. Virgilio P. Elizondo, Ph. D., S. T. D.

William H. Sadlier, Inc.
9 Pine Street
New York, New York 10005-1002
http://www.sadlier.com

CONTENTS

Unit 1   Living as a Catholic Christian   page

Doctrine: Catholic Teaching   **Faith Alive at Home and in the Parish**

| Unit 4 | We Live as Christians | page |

Doctrine: Catholic Teaching **Faith Alive at Home and in the Parish**

DEAR YOUNG PEOPLE,

Your new religion book is called **Coming to God's Love.** It is written to help you grow in living as a friend of Jesus Christ and a member of his Church.

Coming to God's Love tells how the commandments of God and the teachings of Jesus Christ help us to live happily and freely as God's people.

It teaches us that we share the responsibility for building the kingdom, or reign, of God in our world today.

When you use this book, ask the Holy Spirit to help you to

- be a faithful follower of Jesus Christ;
- live faithfully the commandments of God and of the Church;
- find ways that you can be a sign of God's love to everyone;
- thank God by your words and actions for the gift of his love;
- think about ways Jesus wants you to continue his work and be a peacemaker.

We hope that you will enjoy learning how God wants us to live. We pray that you will continue to grow in God's love always.

All of Us in the Sadlier Family

Called by Name

OUR LIFE

Think for a minute. What does it mean for you to have a name?

Your parents probably thought and talked about many names before they chose the one that was to be yours. Why is a name so important? Wouldn't a number do just as well?

How do you feel about your name?

HELLO MY NAME IS:

HELLO MY NAME IS:

ELISA

HELLO MY NAME IS:

Paul

SHARING LIFE

Each one of us here has a name that is ours alone. How many people in our group can you name?

Stand in a circle. Take turns walking around the inside of the circle. When the music stops, or when your catechist says to stop, the "walker" must find out and name the person in front of him or her. Everyone else in the circle should repeat the name correctly and with respect.

7

In the Gospel of Luke we read the wonderful story about the angel Gabriel coming from God to ask Mary to be the mother of the Savior. The angel said to Mary, "Hail, favored one! The Lord is with you. . . . You will . . . bear a son, and you shall name him Jesus."
Luke 1:28,31

The name Jesus means "God saves." Jesus came to save and to give new life to all people. Whenever we say the name of Jesus, we remember that he is our Savior. This is the reason we show great respect for the holy name of Jesus. We never use this name except in saying our prayers or in sharing our faith.

Each of us has an individual name that identifies who we are. These are the very names by which God calls us. In the Bible we read, "I have called you by name: you are mine" (Isaiah 43:1).

We also share a common name that identifies us as disciples of Jesus Christ. We are called Christians; we follow Jesus Christ. We carry his name to identify who we are.

This year we will learn much more about what it means to follow Jesus Christ in the Church. We will grow together in following his way and in living for the kingdom of God.

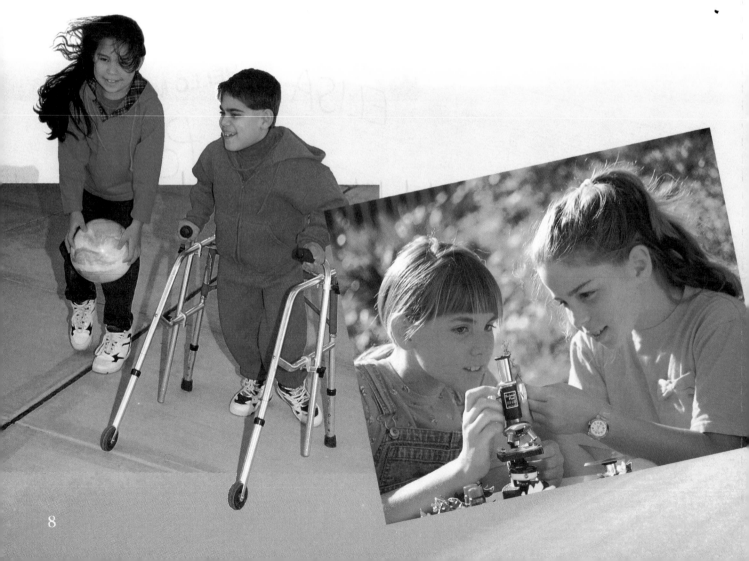

At the World Youth Day in Denver, Colorado, Pope John Paul II spoke to young people from all over the world about what it means to be a follower of Jesus Christ. He said:

"Young people from every corner of the world, you have opened your hearts to the truth of Christ's promise of new life. You, young pilgrims, have also shown that you understand that Christ's gift of life is not for you alone. . . . Place your intelligence, your talents, your enthusiasm, your compassion, and your strength at the service of life!"

From "A Celebration of Life,"
Pope John Paul II

To follow Jesus means:

- to cherish and care for the gift of your own life;

- to defend and support the lives of other people;

- to live your life following the example of Jesus.

This year we will be "pilgrims"— people on a journey with Jesus Christ. We will explore ways that we can use our intelligence, our enthusiasm, our concern for others, and our strengths to live and share the life that Jesus our Savior came to give to all people.

COMING TO FAITH

You are a Christian. Talk together about what the name Christian means to you. Create a personal symbol or word that shows what it means to you to be a disciple of Jesus Christ.

PRACTICING FAITH

Come together in a prayer circle and take turns sharing your symbols. Then pray together:

† Jesus, you have called us by name. We are yours. We want to be your disciples and to share your life with our world.

Now make a garland of your symbols by pasting them, one by one, on a long piece of yarn or string.

Keep your garland in a place where you will see it next time you meet.

Talk with your catechist about ways you and your family can share the "Faith Alive" pages. Talk to your family about your Christian message. Maybe other family members would like to write their own.

This year your son or daughter will explore in depth what it means to live as a disciple of Jesus. He or she will learn what it means to follow Him by living as a member of the Catholic Church. Within the Church community we support one another in following the way of Jesus by living according to the Ten Commandments, the Law of Love, the Beatitudes, and the Works of Mercy. You will want to continue to take an active role in guiding your child's growth in Christian faith. Here are some ways *Coming to God's Love* might assist you.

■ Talk about each lesson together, including the pictures and artwork, if possible, since they are an essential part of the program. Encourage a conversation about the *Faith Summary* statements. The symbol reminds you to help your child learn *Faith Summary* statements by heart. Remember that "learning by heart" may include but means much more than memorization. It means taking and making these statements one's own, taking them into one's heart. You might ask a question for each statement to prompt your child's response. Be sensitive since not every child has equal facility with memorization. It is more important that your child have the faith statements in his or her heart.

■ Invite your child to share with you any songs, poems, or experiences of prayer that have been learned or shared. Even before truths of our Catholic faith are fully understood, they can be appropriated through a favorite song or prayer.

■ Use the *Faith Alive at Home and in the Parish* pages (this is the first of them) to continue and to expand your child's catechesis through the experience of the community of faith in your family and in the parish family. There will be a great variety of activities on these pages. Try to do at least one with your fourth grader.

The **Family Scripture Moment** is offered as a unique opportunity for the family to share faith by "breaking open" God's word together. The "moment" can be as brief or as long as you wish. The following simple outline is one way to use this faith time together.

■ **Gather** together as a family. All can participate from the youngest to the oldest.

■ **Listen** to God's word as it is read, slowly and expressively, by a family member.

■ **Share** what you hear from the reading that touches your own life. Give time for each one to do this.

■ **Consider** the points suggested for family enrichment as a way to come to a deeper understanding of God's word.

■ **Reflect** on and then share any new understandings.

■ **Decide** as a family ways you will try to live God's word.

In this fourth-grade text, selected passages from the letters, or epistles, of the New Testament will be suggested for family faith sharing, prayer, and reflection.

Learn by heart **Faith Summary**

- We are called Christians because we are disciples of Jesus Christ.

- We are called to share Jesus' life with others.

- We show respect for the holy name of Jesus.

A Christian Message

Think about what it means to say, "I am a Christian." Pretend you and your friends set up a toll-free phone line, 1-800-CHRISTIAN. What message would you record on your machine that tells people what it means to be a Christian?

Take a few minutes to go over the *Faith Summary* together. To help your fourth grader learn the summary by heart, you might want to ask a question for each statement. Pay particular attention to the second and third statements.

Faith Word Wheel

Make a faith wheel like the sample. Cut out a large circle from heavy paper. Divide the circle (front and back) into numbered sections. For each lesson write a faith word on the front. On the back write its meaning. Keep your wheel in a special place to remind you of what you have learned.

FAMILY SCRIPTURE MOMENT

Gather and ask: What are some of the things that make us joyful and thankful? Do we ever thank God for any of our troubles? Why or why not? Then **Listen** to an encouraging message from Saint Paul, who wrote many letters to the first Christians.

Rejoice always. Pray without ceasing. In all circumstances give thanks, for this is the will of God for you in Christ Jesus. Do not quench the Spirit. Do not despise prophetic utterances. Test everything; retain what is good. Refrain from every kind of evil. May the God of peace himself make you perfectly holy and may you entirely, spirit, soul, and body, be preserved blameless for the coming of our Lord Jesus Christ.

1 Thessalonians 5:16–23

Share which piece of advice is most meaningful for each family member.

Consider for family enrichment:

■ Paul's letter to the new Christians of the Greek city of Thessalonica shows his desire to see them grow in holiness by living their faith.

■ Our Christian faith should be a source of joy for us. When we listen to the Holy Spirit, we know that we are doing what God wants.

Reflect What would it mean for us as a family to listen to the Holy Spirit?

Decide How will we celebrate and show this week our joy as Christians?

1 Living for God's Kingdom

Our Life

Every day we hear bad news and good news about our world. What bad news have you heard recently? What good news?

Pretend you are a TV reporter. The TV camera is focused on these two pictures. Give a report of what is happening in each scene.

Sharing Life

Talk together about ways the bad things in our world might be changed to good things.

Do you think they can be changed? Why or why not?

Imagine Jesus is sitting in our group right now. What do you think he might say to us about the good and bad things in our world?

The Kingdom of God

When Jesus was about thirty years old, he left his home to begin his mission, or task, of preaching his good news to the world.

The good news Jesus preached was that God loves all people and that the kingdom of God had come in him.

One Sabbath day Jesus went to the synagogue in Nazareth. When invited to read, he found and then read this passage from the Scriptures:

"The Spirit of the Lord is upon me,
    because he has anointed me
        to bring glad tidings to the poor.
He has sent me to proclaim liberty
        to captives
    and recovery of sight to the blind,
        to let the oppressed go free,
    and to proclaim a year acceptable
        to the Lord."

Then Jesus said, "Today this scripture passage is fulfilled in your hearing."

Everyone was amazed. Jesus was saying that this great Scripture reading had come true in him. The people began to whisper to one another, "Isn't this the son of Joseph?" They did not believe that Jesus was the Son of God, sent by God the Father to bring about God's kingdom of justice and peace.
Based on Luke 4:16–22

The kingdom, or reign, of God is the saving power of God's life and love in the world. It is the good news that God loves us and is always with us. God does not want any people to be hungry, hurting, or treated unfairly.

We Live for the Kingdom

Jesus went from place to place, telling everyone how to live for the kingdom of God. He often used parables, or stories, to help his listeners understand what the kingdom of God was like. Here is one parable that Jesus told about the kingdom:

The kingdom of God is like a treasure hidden in a field. When someone finds this treasure, that person sells everything to buy the field. Then the person owns the most valuable treasure of all.

Based on Matthew 13:44

This parable helps us to understand that doing God's loving will must come first in our lives.

When Jesus talked about the kingdom of God, some did not understand what he really meant. They thought that he was talking about a country or a kingdom where Jesus would be an earthly king.

The **kingdom,** or **reign,** of **God** is the saving power of God's life and love in the world.

Jesus tells us that the kingdom of God is not a place. It is living so that all who see us know what it means to do God's loving will. God's will is what is best for us and what he wants for us here and now.

Jesus has promised us that even the smallest thing we do for the kingdom of God will make a difference in ourselves and in our world.

We can build up God's kingdom by:
- believing the good news.
- following Jesus.
- avoiding sin.
- loving others and ourselves.
- working for justice and peace in our world.

15

COMING TO FAITH

We are followers of Jesus Christ. We are called to help build up the kingdom of God.

What can fourth graders do to:

- share the good news of Jesus?

- work for justice?

- be peacemakers?

PRACTICING FAITH

Go on a treasure hunt to find the real meaning of the kingdom of God. Draw a dotted line to show the route your ship will take. Avoid the things that will keep you from the kingdom. Stop at the things that will help you reach your goal. After the treasure hunt, gather together and pray the Our Father.

Treasure of the Kingdom of God

caring for God's gifts

making peace

fighting

making fun of someone

helping at home

disobeying rules

Start

Talk with your catechist about ways you and your family can use the "Faith Alive" pages together, especially the activity on the kingdom of God.

FAITH ALIVE AT HOME AND IN THE PARISH

In this lesson your son or daughter learned that we as disciples of Jesus Christ are called to bring about the kingdom, or reign, of God. Invite your child to tell you what was learned for his or her own life.

Talk to your family about the fact that each member can live for God's reign by doing his loving and life-giving will. We do God's will by working with love and by working for justice, peace, and fullness of life for all.

Make a list of loving things that are done in your home and neighborhood. These are signs of the presence of God's reign. At the top of the paper write, "We know that God's kingdom is here because...." Ask each family member to add to the list during the week.

Pictures of Our World

Set up a bulletin board at home on the theme, "Keeping the Kingdom of God." Each week cut out pictures or stories from newspapers or magazines that show people who are working together to bring about the reign of God.

Kingdom of God Report

To help your child understand God's kingdom better, ask him or her to create a bottled message to tell someone on a deserted island about something that Jesus said about the kingdom of God.

† Family Prayer

Pray the Our Father with your child to ask God's help in doing his will for justice and peace, love and life for all.

Jesus said the kingdom of God is like

_____

_____

_____

_____

_____

_____

_____

_____

_____

_____

Faith Summary

- Jesus preached the good news of the kingdom of God.

- The kingdom of God is the saving power of God's life and love in the world.

- We build up the kingdom of God by working for love, justice, and peace in our world.

17

Go over the *Faith Summary* together and encourage your child to learn it by heart, especially the second statement. Then have your fourth grader complete the *Review*. The answers to questions 1–4 appear on page 216. The response to number 5 will show how well your fourth grader understands that God's kingdom comes about when people do God's will. When the *Review* is completed, go over it together.

Cross out the phrase that does NOT belong.

1. Jesus preached about

   a. the kingdom of God.

   b. God's love.

   c. the geography of Palestine.

2. Jesus said the kingdom of God was

   a. like a treasure hidden in a field.

   b. a country with a king.

   c. living the good news.

3. The kingdom of God means that

   a. God is present in our lives.

   b. God loves us always.

   c. God's kingdom is a country.

4. To belong to God's kingdom we must

   a. turn away from sin.

   b. do God's will.

   c. do nothing.

5. How can everyone help to bring about the kingdom of God?

_____

_____

FAMILY SCRIPTURE MOMENT

Gather and invite family members to share some good news they have received recently. Then **Listen** to Saint Paul's description of the good news of Jesus Christ.

Paul, …called to be an apostle and set apart for the gospel of God, which he promised previously through his prophets in the holy scriptures, the gospel about his Son, descended from David according to the flesh, but established as Son of God in power according to the spirit of holiness through resurrection from the dead, Jesus Christ our Lord. Through him we have received the grace of apostleship….

Romans 1:2–5

Share What is Paul's central idea of the good news of Jesus? How does this good news affect our attitudes and daily actions?

Consider for family enrichment:

■ Paul paves the way for his first visit to the Christian community at Rome by assuring them that the risen Christ is the "content" of the good news he comes to share with them.

■ Jesus Christ is both human and divine. He is the Son of God and human like us. He must always be the center of our Christian faith.

Reflect and **Decide** What might it mean for us to be good news for others? How will we as a family communicate the good news of Jesus to someone who especially needs it this week?

Loving God, help us to trust in you.

OUR LIFE

"Loving God, teach me to trust in you." This was the prayer of a great saint, Teresa of Avila. It is a prayer that we, too, can pray often.

Teresa lived in Spain in the 16th century. She was beautiful, friendly, bright—and funny, too. She blended great reverence with down-to-earth honesty in her conversations with God. She often let God know when he seemed to be asking a lot of her. Yet she drew strength from his presence in her life and in the world around her. Everything in nature spoke to Teresa of God's presence and love. In one of her prayers she wrote:

"O God, how you show forth your power in giving courage to a little ant!"

What do you think Teresa saw an ant doing that caused her to praise God?

Do you ever find signs that God is present in the world? What are they?

SHARING LIFE

What do you think is the best way to show trust in God?

What are some things that make it hard to trust in God?

Faith in God

We can always trust a loving parent. Even more so, we can always believe and trust in God. God will always love us and care for us.

Jesus explained why we can have such faith in God. Jesus said, "Look at the birds in the sky; they do not sow or reap. . . , yet your heavenly Father feeds them. Are not you more important than they?"
Based on Matthew 6:26

Jesus then showed how God cares for us as a loving parent cares for a child. Jesus told them that their Father in heaven knows all that they need and would care for them.
Based on Matthew 6:32–33

When we have faith in God, we believe and trust in God who loves and cares for us. Having faith helps us to make good choices so that we live as disciples of Jesus Christ.

Hope in God

We must also have hope in God. Hope helps us never to give up, no matter what happens to us, our family, or our world. Our faith gives us this confidence, or strong trust, in God's love.

Christians also have hope that God will give us eternal life. *Eternal life* means living forever with God in heaven.

A **virtue** is the habit of doing good.

Love of God

Jesus always taught people how to love God, one another, and themselves. He said that the commandment to love was the greatest teaching of the Scriptures: "You shall love the Lord, your God, with all your heart, with all your being, with all your strength, and with all your mind, and your neighbor as yourself."
Based on Luke 10:27

This teaching is called the Law of Love. The Law of Love means that we treat every person as our neighbor. It also means that we share this message of love with others by the example of our own lives. Christians must try to show this love especially to people who are hungry, poor, or treated unjustly.

Faith, hope, and love are gifts from God. They are called virtues. A virtue is the habit of doing good. Faith, hope, and love are the greatest virtues in a Christian's life.

Like all habits, we do not learn to practice the virtues of faith, hope, and love overnight. But Jesus expects us to keep on trying to live them. Beginning again is more important than counting how many times we fail.

21

Coming To Faith

Imagine you are standing among God's gifts of nature. Sit in a relaxed position and feel God's presence and love. Finish the prayer.

† Jesus, help my faith to be as strong as. . . .

Jesus, help my hope in God to be as tall as. . . .

Jesus, help my love for God to flow as deep as. . . .

Practicing Faith

Sit in a circle with your group. One at a time hold a small smooth rock in the palm of your hand. Rub it gently. To help you feel at peace, turn the rock over and over slowly in the palm of your hands. Choose one of the statements below and complete it. Then pass the rock to your neighbor. Listen carefully as each of your friends completes a chosen statement.

My faith gives me strength to. . . .

My greatest hope for myself is. . . .

For me, love is most difficult when. . . .

Talk with your catechist about ways you and your family might use the "Faith Alive" pages. You and a family member might want to do the Scripture activity together. Pray the Act of Faith with your catechist and friends.

FAITH ALIVE AT HOME AND IN THE PARISH

 In this lesson your fourth grader has learned about the great Christian virtues of faith, hope, and love—the theological virtues. We call these three virtues "theological" because they are gifts of God, lead us to God, and help us to live in a deeper relationship with the Blessed Trinity. The image of God as a loving father was reinforced. Your child needs to see God in you and to experience these great virtues being practiced in your home. Talk as a family about ways each of you will practice these virtues better this week. Ask yourself how you can be a more "loving parent" to your child.

God's Love and Care

Help your fourth grader understand the importance of trust that God cares for us as a loving parent.

Read the Scripture passage below and discuss its meaning with your family. Use a basket or a bowl to make a nest. Keep the nest as a reminder of God's love and protection for you. Write and place Scripture quotes in the "nest." For example: Matthew 6:26; Isaiah 31:5; Hosea 14:4–8; Psalm 23:1– 4; John 15:1–10. Each day this week choose one to pray.

† Pray an Act of Faith

O God, we believe all that Jesus has taught us about you. We place all our trust in you because of your great love for us.

† Pray an Act of Hope

O God, we never give up on your love. We have hope and will work for your kingdom to come and for a life that lasts forever with you in heaven.

† Pray an Act of Love

O God, we love you above all things. Help us to love ourselves and one another as Jesus taught us to do.

Just as a bird hovers over its nest to protect its young, so I, your God, will protect you.

Based on Isaiah 31:5

Learn by heart

Faith Summary

- Faith enables us to believe and trust in God.

- Hope enables us to have full confidence in God, no matter what happens.

- Love enables us to love God, ourselves, and our neighbors.

Go over the *Faith Summary* together and encourage your child to learn all three statements by heart. Then help your fourth grader complete the *Review.* The answers to numbers 1–4 appear on page 216. The response to number 5 will show how well your fourth grader is making the connection between practicing faith, hope, and love and being Jesus' disciple. When the *Review* is completed, go over it together.

Circle the letter beside the correct answer.

1. Jesus shows us

   a. how to care only for ourselves.

   b. that God will always love us.

   c. how to be the most popular person.

2. To have faith means to

   a. believe and trust in God.

   b. always make the easy choice.

   c. believe in magic.

3. Hope means that

   a. we have no problems.

   b. we have just what we want.

   c. we never give up on God's love.

4. A habit of doing good is called

   a. the Law of Love.

   b. a virtue.

   c. a work of mercy.

5. How will people know that you are Jesus' disciple?

_____

_____

FAMILY SCRIPTURE MOMENT

Gather and ask each person: What is true love for you? Now **Listen** as a family to Saint Paul's tribute to true love.

If I speak in human and angelic tongues but do not have love, I am a resounding gong or a clashing cymbal. Love is patient, love is kind. It is not jealous, [love] is not pompous, it is not inflated, it is not rude, it does not seek its own interests, it is not quick-tempered, it does not brood over injury, it does not rejoice over wrongdoing but rejoices with the truth. It bears all things, believes all things, hopes all things, endures all things. Love never fails. So, faith, hope, love remain, these three; but the greatest of these is love.

1 Corinthians 13:1, 4–8, 13

Share what each person thinks of Paul's description of true love. Ask: How do we show one another the kind of love that "never gives up"?

Consider for family enrichment:

◼ Paul's "love letter" to the Christians of Corinth challenges them to practice the highest and most lasting virtue that people can achieve.

◼ Paul's description is the ideal standard of love that always challenges the disciples of Jesus.

Reflect and **Decide** Invite each person to choose one "love is" or "love is not" line from Paul's description. Talk about trying to practice it one day at a time.

3 The Church, Jesus' Community

Our Life

Simon (later called Peter), his brother Andrew, and their partners James and John had been fishing all night in the Sea of Galilee. They caught nothing.

Then Jesus came along and told them to try again. They did, and soon the boats were so filled with fish that they were almost sinking. Jesus said, "Do not be afraid; from now on you will be catching men."

Simon, Andrew, James, and John quickly pulled the boats up on the beach. Then they left everything and followed Jesus, becoming his disciples.
Based on Luke 5:1–11

Why did Simon and his friends follow Jesus?

What is it about Jesus that makes you want to follow him?

Sharing Life

Imagine you are with Simon Peter on the day that Jesus said, "Come, follow me." What might Jesus be asking you to do?

Can you follow Jesus today? How?

Filled with the Spirit

Jesus knew that Peter and his other followers would need help to live as his disciples. At the Last Supper, Jesus told his disciples that he would send them a Helper. Jesus said, "The Advocate, the holy Spirit, that the Father will send in my name—he will teach you everything and remind you of all that [I] told you."
John 14:26

On the following day, Good Friday, Jesus was put to death on a cross. Many of his friends were so afraid that they ran away to hide. Three days later their fear turned into joy. Jesus was alive. Jesus had risen from the dead!

After forty days, Jesus returned to his Father in heaven. Jesus' friends were together with Mary, his mother. All at once they heard a noise like a loud wind blowing. They saw what looked like tongues of fire spread out and touch each person. They were all filled with God the Holy Spirit, as Jesus promised.

Now the disciples of Jesus went forth as his witnesses. With courage, they told everyone the good news about Jesus. Many people were baptized. This is how our Church began to grow. We call this day the feast of Pentecost.

The Church Today

Today the Church is guided by God the Holy Spirit. The Church still carries on the work of Jesus, as the first Christians did. The Church preaches and lives the good news of God's kingdom. It tells people all over the world that God loves us and is near to us.

Our Church is also a community of worship. We gather together to praise and thank God, our source of life and love. All over the world, our Church celebrates Mass and the sacraments. Our Church continues Jesus' work of serving and caring for others, especially people most in need. Today our Church reaches out to everyone and welcomes all people into Jesus' community. We try to live as a community of faith, hope and love.

We Belong to the Church

We become members of the Church through Baptism. By this sacrament we are freed from the power of sin, become children of God, and are welcomed into the Church, the body of Christ. Our Baptism and our membership in the Church helps us to overcome the effects of original sin and to live as God's children in the world.

We are to love and care for one another, as Jesus teaches us. Our parish is a community made up of all the families and other people in our neighborhood who belong to the Catholic Church. Together we worship God and live for his kingdom. We care for one another and for those who do not belong to the Church. We share the good news of Jesus and work for justice and peace.

All the Catholic parishes in one area make up a diocese, which is led by the bishop. All the dioceses together make up the Catholic Church, which is found throughout the whole world.

27

Coming To Faith

Tell how the Holy Spirit helps us in our Church to be witnesses for Jesus. Share how we spread the good news, worship, and serve others.

Then share with one another how belonging to the Church makes a difference in your life.

Practicing Faith

Work with a partner. Choose one of these words that tells what the Church does: **WITNESS; WORSHIP; SERVE.** See whether you can create an acrostic that tells what it means to you. Here is an example:

We spread the good news.

I am a member of the Church.

The Church continues Jesus' work.

Newness of life comes from the Holy Spirit.

Everyone is welcome in our Church.

Spirit-filled, the Church is found throughout the world.

Serving others is one way to witness.

Share your acrostics. Then pray together:

† God the Holy Spirit, give us the courage to be Jesus' witnesses.

Talk with your catechist about ways you and your family can use the "Faith Alive" pages. Work with your family to decide how you will continue Jesus' mission. Then share the blessing ceremony with your group.

FAITH ALIVE AT HOME AND IN THE PARISH

In this lesson your fourth grader learned how the Church began and what it means to belong to the Church today. The Holy Spirit guides and empowers the Church to continue the prophetic ministry of Jesus in every age. The Spirit helps us today in the same way that the first Christians were helped to witness to their faith.

Your child has also learned that first of all we belong to the Church in our families. Every family has the mission of witnessing, worshiping, building community, sharing God's word, and serving as Jesus did.

Have your fourth grader tell you the story of Jesus calling Simon Peter and the other apostles to follow him. Then talk about ways your family can follow Jesus and continue his mission.

Continuing Jesus' Mission

Plan together ways your family will witness to the good news, worship God, or serve others this week. In the space below decide together how to continue Jesus' mission.

Our Decision:

_____

_____

_____

† A Family Blessing

Commission your family as a "little Church." If possible, use holy water in this blessing ceremony.

Leader: We are gathered together as a family with Jesus in our midst. I bless each of you with this holy water.

All: Jesus, fill (name) with your love. Help us to follow your way and to share our faith with others. May our hearts and our home be filled with your life. Amen.

Learn by heart Faith Summary

- The Church is guided by the Holy Spirit.

- The Church preaches, serves, worships, and lives as Jesus' community of faith, hope, and love.

- We become members of the Church through Baptism.

Go over the *Faith Summary* together and encourage your child to learn it by heart, especially the second and third statements. Then have your fourth grader complete the *Review*.

The answers to numbers 1–4 appear on page 216. The response to number 5 will help you to see how well your fourth grader understands what it means to live as a disciple of Jesus. When the *Review* is completed, go over it together.

Circle the letter beside the correct answer.

1. Jesus wanted his disciples to live

    a. in Jerusalem.

    b. as a community.

    c. in the same place.

2. The Church lives as Jesus showed by

    a. serving all people.

    b. serving only certain people.

    c. neither of the above.

3. The Church worships God

    a. on Sundays only.

    b. whenever we praise God.

    c. in our parish church only.

4. We belong to the Church in

    a. our family only.

    b. our parish only.

    c. our family, our parish, and the whole Church all over the world.

5. Jesus invites you to be his disciple. Tell how you will answer him this week.

_____

_____

FAMILY SCRIPTURE MOMENT

Gather and ask each family member what it means to belong to God. Then **Listen** as a family to Saint Paul.

In him we were also chosen, destined in accord with the purpose of the One who accomplishes all things according to the intention of his will…. In him you also, who have heard the word of truth, the gospel of your salvation, and have believed in him, were sealed with the promised holy Spirit, which is the first installment of our inheritance towards redemption as God's possession, to the praise of his glory.
Ephesians 1:11, 13–14

Share times when we think God the Holy Spirit is most present in our lives. Then each one

responds to this question: What promises do I feel that God has made to me?

Consider for family enrichment:

■ As a faith community, we have been chosen by God to belong to God. By Baptism each of us has received the Holy Spirit, the "guarantee" of all that God promises us.

■ To be God's holy people, we must believe in Christ. We do this in the Holy Spirit, who helps us to live our faith.

Reflect and **Decide** How might the Holy Spirit be urging our parish to grow? What will we do as a family to show that we have been "stamped" by the Holy Spirit and belong to God?

4 The Beatitudes

Lord, teach us to find true happiness in doing your will.

OUR LIFE

Once upon a time there was a very rich king called Midas. He was the richest man in the world, but he was not happy. He wanted more.

One day, as he sadly counted his gold, a stranger suddenly appeared before him. "Why are you sad, King Midas?" asked the stranger.

Midas said, "I wish everything I owned were gold."

"You shall have your wish," the stranger said.

The next morning when Midas awoke, he touched his blanket. It turned to gold! So did his clothes and his furniture! Midas was deliriously happy.

He had the golden touch! Suddenly his little daughter came running to him. She threw her arms around him and kissed him. She became a beautiful golden statue.

Finish the story and share your endings with one another. What do you think of Midas' wish and its results?

SHARING LIFE

If you could wish for something that would make you most happy, what would it be? Why?

Imagine what Jesus would wish for us. Share your ideas as a group.

Our Catholic Faith

True Happiness

People sometimes think that having a lot of money or possessions or being famous will make them happy. Jesus taught that true happiness comes from doing God's loving will. One day Jesus began to teach the people how to be truly happy. He taught them the Beatitudes. Here are the eight Beatitudes and what they mean.

The Beatitudes

Blessed are the poor in spirit,
 for theirs is the kingdom of heaven.

Blessed are they who mourn,
 for they will be comforted.

Blessed are the meek,
 for they will inherit the land.

Blessed are they who hunger and
  thirst for righteousness,
 for they will be satisfied.

Blessed are the merciful,
 for they will be shown mercy.

Blessed are the clean of heart,
 for they will see God.

Blessed are the peacemakers,
 for they will be called children of God.

Blessed are those who are persecuted . . .
 for theirs is the kingdom of heaven.

Matthew 5:3–10

The Beatitudes are the spirit of love, peace, justice, mercy, and generosity required of Jesus' disciples. They remind us that in living for God's kingdom, we find true happiness.

It is not easy to live the way of the Beatitudes. We need courage to choose to live this way. But the Holy Spirit is with us and helps us live as Jesus' disciples.

What They Mean

People who are poor in spirit depend on God for everything. Nothing becomes more important to them than God.

People who are saddened by sin, evil, and suffering in the world but trust that God will comfort them.

Humble people show gentleness and patience toward others. They will share in God's promises.

People who are fair and just towards others are doing God's loving will.

Merciful people are concerned about others' feelings. They are willing to forgive those who hurt them.

People who keep God first in their lives are pure in heart. They give their worries and concerns to God.

Peacemakers are people who bring peace and reconciliation into the lives of others. They treat others fairly.

People who are willing to be ignored or insulted for doing what they feel God wants will share in his kingdom.

FAITH WORD

The **Beatitudes** are ways of living that Jesus gave us so that we can be truly happy.

33

COMING TO FAITH

Do you think it takes courage to live with the spirit of love, peace, justice, mercy, and generosity that the Beatitudes teach? Explain.

Explain why you think Jesus calls these people "happy."

- the peacemakers
- the merciful
- those who work for justice

PRACTICING FAITH

Form two teams. Each team will draw up eight "Who am I?" Beatitude questions. Each team will challenge the other to name the Beatitude. For example:

I call you to do what God wants even when people make fun of you or insult you. Who am I? (eighth Beatitude)

Pray together.

† Jesus, help us to be Beatitude people— people who work for peace, love, justice, mercy, and care for those in need. Then we will truly know the happiness of God's kingdom.

Close by reading aloud each Beatitude together slowly and prayerfully.

Talk with your catechist about ways you and your family might use the "Faith Alive" pages. You might especially want to pray a Beatitude together.

34

FAITH ALIVE AT HOME AND IN THE PARISH

In this lesson your fourth grader learned that the Beatitudes taught by Jesus are ways of living a happy life. Scripture scholars tell us that these sayings were probably frequent and central aspects of Jesus' preaching. Let your child tell you what each Beatitude means to him or her.

Living the Beatitudes brings happiness and peace to your family. Our bishops teach us that when we speak up for others who are being treated unfairly, we are peacemakers.

But peace does not just happen. We must work for peace among members of our family, in our parish, and in our world. Moved by compassion, we bring peace to our family by making up, or being reconciled, with anyone with whom we are angry.

Learn by heart ## Faith Summary

- The Beatitudes teach us how to follow Jesus and be truly happy.

- The Holy Spirit helps us to live the Beatitudes.

- The Beatitudes are the spirit of love, mercy, and generosity required of Jesus' disciples.

Living the Beatitudes

Think about ways you and your family can live the Beatitudes this week.

- Be willing to forgive when we are wronged.

- Help someone whom others are making fun of or ignoring.

- Speak up for others who are being treated unfairly.

- _____

- _____

- _____

- _____

- _____

† Family Prayer

Help your family learn how living the Beatitudes brings happiness and peace. Choose a Beatitude. Say it together as a family, and decide how you will live it this week.

Go over the *Faith Summary* together and encourage your child to learn it by heart, especially the first statement. Then help your fourth grader complete the *Review.* The answers to numbers 1–4 appear on page 216. The response to number 5 will help you to discuss with your fourth grader how to live the Beatitudes. When the *Review* is completed, go over it together.

Answer the following questions.

1. Who will receive what God has promised?

_____

_____

2. Who comforts those who mourn?

_____

_____

3. Who are called the children of God?

_____

_____

4. Who will see God?

_____

_____

5. How will you be merciful to others this week?

_____

_____

FAMILY SCRIPTURE MOMENT

Gather and ask: Who are our heroes? How do they contribute to the happiness of others? Then **Listen** as Saint Paul describes Christian heroes and heroines.

In everything we commend ourselves as ministers of God, through much endurance, in afflictions, hardships, constraints, … by purity, knowledge, patience, kindness, in a holy spirit, in unfeigned love, in truthful speech, in the power of God;…through glory and dishonor, insult and praise. We are treated as deceivers and yet are truthful; as unrecognized and yet acknowledged; as dying and behold we live; as chastised and yet not put to death; as sorrowful yet always rejoicing; as poor yet enriching many; as having nothing and yet possessing all things.
2 Corinthians 6:4, 6–10

Share In what ways do we hope to be heroes in the eyes of God?

Consider for family enrichment:

■ Paul assures the persecuted Christians of Corinth that their faithful service of God is a lasting source of inner wealth and happiness.

■ We "possess everything" that really matters when we live by our Christian faith.

Reflect and **Decide** How might we make others rich by sharing our Christian faith?

5 Living as Our Best Selves

Jesus, help us to remember that whatever we do for others, we do for you.

to be continued....

Our Life

One day Jesus told the parable of the Good Samaritan.

A man was traveling from Jerusalem to Jericho. Suddenly a gang attacked him, beat him badly, and took everything he had. They left him lying in a ditch, half dead.

Soon a priest from the Temple came along the road. He saw the man but walked by on the other side of the road. Then a Levite came by. He went over and looked at the man but then kept on going.

Finally a Samaritan, a foreigner and someone hated in Israel, came upon the man. He stopped, gently lifted the man and cared for his wounds. Then he put the man on his donkey and took him to an inn. He gave the innkeeper money, saying, "Take care of him. . . . I shall repay you on my way back."
Based on Luke 10:30–35

Which person do you think acted as a neighbor to the man?

What do you hear Jesus saying for your life?

Sharing Life

Did you ever help someone who didn't expect your help? Tell about it.

Who are some "good Samaritans" in our world today?

Do you have to know someone in order to be a "neighbor" to them? Explain.

The Works of Mercy

Jesus taught his disciples how he wanted them to live. One day he told a large crowd that he would come again at the end of the world to judge everyone. At this last judgment, the Lord will separate people into two groups, just as a shepherd separates the sheep from the goats. To the first group on his right, he will say, "Come, you who are blessed by my Father. Inherit the kingdom prepared for you from the foundation of the world."

- I was hungry and you gave me food, I was thirsty and you gave me drink.

- I was a stranger and you welcomed me, naked and you clothed me.

- I was ill and you cared for me, in prison and you visited me.

These people will say, "Lord, when did we ever do any of these for you?"

Jesus will say, "I say to you, whatever you did for one of these least brothers of mine, you did for me."

Then Jesus will turn to the other people and say, "What you did not do for one of these least ones, you did not do for me." Jesus will say to these people, "Depart from me."

These people, "the goats," will be sent into the eternal punishment of hell. The others, "the sheep," who did God's will, shall receive eternal life in heaven.

Based on Matthew 25:31–46

Heaven is being with God and the friends of God forever.

The Catholic Church teaches us ways to help us care for the physical needs of others. They are called the Corporal Works of Mercy. *Corporal* refers to what our bodies need to be healthy and well.

To help us care for the spiritual needs of people, the Catholic Church teaches us the Spiritual Works of Mercy.

The Corporal Works of Mercy

- Feed the hungry.
- Give drink to the thirsty.
- Clothe the naked.
- Help those imprisoned.
- Shelter the homeless.
- Care for the sick.
- Bury the dead.

The Spiritual Works of Mercy

- Share your knowledge with others.
- Give advice to those who need it.
- Comfort those who suffer.
- Be patient with people.
- Forgive those who hurt us.
- Give correction to those who need it.
- Pray for the living and the dead.

When we are just and merciful, we live as God wants us to live. We live the way of the kingdom of God.

COMING TO FAITH

Have one group act out the story of the Good Samaritan. Choose someone to narrate the story as others act the parts.

End by asking, as Jesus did, "Who was neighbor to the man?"

Then have another group act out Jesus' story of the last judgment.

Ask one another: Why is it Jesus himself for whom we are caring when we do the Works of Mercy?

PRACTICING FAITH

Talk with a friend about one way you can practice a Work of Mercy this week.

Decide when and how you will do it. Share your decision with the group.

End by praying the Family Prayer as a group.

Talk with your catechist about ways you and your family can use the "Faith Alive" pages together. Maybe your family can help you fulfill your work of mercy this week.

FAITH ALIVE AT HOME AND IN THE PARISH

In this lesson your fourth grader learned that Jesus taught us how we will be judged as his disciples. Jesus was never stronger in his teaching than when he spoke about the ways we must care for others. The beautiful parable of the Good Samaritan and the parable of the Last Judgment make it very clear what our responsibilities are in living our faith. As a family, help one another to see that the Corporal and Spiritual Works of Mercy are ways to live for the kingdom of God. See how well your child can explain them to you. Talk about their importance for your family.

A Good Samaritan Today

Using the worksheet below, ask each family member to choose and practice one Work of Mercy this week. Help your child to learn the Works of Mercy by heart.

> Name someone you know who acts like the Good Samaritan. Describe ways this person lives the Works of Mercy in daily life.
>
> _____
>
> _____
>
> _____
>
> _____

HELPING
SHARING
CARING

† Family Prayer

Listen together and reflect on this powerful statement from Micah, a great prophet of justice and peace in the Old Testament:

You have been told. . .
  what the LORD requires of you:
Only to do the right and to love goodness,
  and to walk humbly with your God.
Micah 6:8

Learn by heart Faith Summary

- The Corporal Works of Mercy are ways we care for one another's physical needs.

- The Spiritual Works of Mercy are ways we care for one another's spiritual needs.

- As disciples of Jesus, we must live the Corporal and Spiritual Works of Mercy.

41

Review

Go over the *Faith Summary* together and encourage your child to learn it by heart, especially the third statement. Then help him or her to complete the *Review*. The answers to numbers 1–4 appear on page 216. The response to number 5 will help you to see how well your fourth grader understands that practicing the Works of Mercy will make him or her more merciful. When the *Review* is completed, go over it together.

Complete the following sentences.

1. The _____ Works of Mercy are ways we can care for the physical needs of others.

2. Name the Work of Mercy you are practicing when you collect food for poor people.

_____

_____

3. The _____ Works of Mercy are ways we can care for the spiritual needs of people.

4. What Work of Mercy are you practicing when you don't hold a grudge?

_____

_____

5. Tell how practicing the Works of Mercy will make you more just and merciful.

_____

_____

FAMILY SCRIPTURE MOMENT

Gather and have family members recall the "most generous" deeds they have done or that others have done for them. Then **Listen** as Saint Paul describes Christian love in action.

Since we have gifts that differ according to the grace given to us, let us exercise them. . . . Let love be sincere; hate what is evil, hold on to what is good. Contribute to the needs of the holy ones, exercise hospitality. Bless those who persecute [you], bless and do not curse them.
Romans 12:6, 9, 13–14

Share Ask: What or who helps us to be cheerful givers? What "strangers" are we to welcome?

Consider for family enrichment:

■ Paul advises the Christians of Rome to be kind, charitable, hospitable, and forgiving to friends and enemies alike. This is what it means to live their Christian faith.

■ The real challenge of Christian love is to reach out to strangers and those who are different from us.

Reflect and **Decide** How does this word of God encourage us to become our best selves? What generous work of love will we do together with others in our parish this week?

6 Celebrating Reconciliation

Our Life

One day Jesus was teaching the people in a friend's house. There was a paralyzed man who wanted Jesus to heal him. His friends carried him to the house but because of the crowds they could not get near. So they carried the paralytic to the roof, opened up some tiles, and lowered the man on his mat right down in front of Jesus. When Jesus saw their faith, he said to them, "As for you, your sins are forgiven."

The teachers of the Law were horrified. "Who is this who speaks blasphemies?" they said. "Who but God alone can forgive sins?"

Jesus looked at them. "Which is easier, to say, 'Your sins are forgiven,' or to say 'Rise and walk'?" To show that he had the power to forgive sins, Jesus turned to the paralyzed man and told him to get up, pick up his mat, and go home!

All at once the man got up and went home rejoicing and praising God.
Based on Luke 5:17–25

Why did Jesus both forgive the paralytic's sins and help him to walk again?

How does it feel to be truly forgiven?

Sharing Life

Imagine that you are the paralyzed man. Your friends lower you right in front of Jesus. He smiles at you. He is pleased that you trust him so much. How do you feel when:

- he says you are forgiven?

- he tells you to walk?

- you realize you are both forgiven and cured?

God Always Forgives

As disciples of Jesus Christ, we are called to love and care for one another. We are to live for God's kingdom of justice and peace for all people.

When we live as Jesus taught, we help everyone to know that God is with us now. But we do not always live for God's kingdom or do what he wants us to do. We do not always love God and others as we should. We do not always love ourselves in the right way. Sometimes we sin. We sin when we freely choose to do something that we know is wrong. We disobey God's law on purpose.

God always forgives us if we are sorry and show it. We want the person we have hurt to forgive us. We want God to forgive us, too. We celebrate his forgiveness in the sacrament of Reconciliation.

Preparing for Reconciliation

We prepare for the sacrament of Reconciliation by thanking God for having loved us so much and by examining our conscience. We think about the Ten Commandments, the Law of Love, and the Beatitudes. We ask ourselves whether we have been living the way that Jesus showed us to live. (You can find these on pages 59 and 32.)

We think about the Corporal Works of Mercy and ask ourselves whether we have been caring for people's physical needs. We think about the Spiritual Works of Mercy and ask ourselves whether we have been caring for the spiritual needs of others. (You can review these on page 39.)

We think of the good things we have done and thank God. We ask God to help us to continue living as disciples of Jesus for the kingdom of God.

I'M SORRY

I'M SORR

We think of the good things that we could have done, but did not do. We decide that we will try harder to live for God's kingdom.

We think of the sinful things we may have done. We tell God we are sorry. We promise to try to change our lives and we ask for God's help. We remember to tell the person whom we might have hurt that we are sorry, too.

I'M SORRY

Coming To Faith

Take a few minutes now to think about the ways you have tried to live as a follower of Jesus Christ.

Try to shut out any noises or distractions. Ask yourself how you have tried to do God's loving will by the way you have lived this week.

Thank God for the good things you have done. Ask God to forgive your sins and failings and to help you do better. Now let's pray together.

I'M SORRY

PRACTICING FAITH

A Prayer Service for Forgiveness

Opening Hymn

Joyful, joyful, we adore you,
God of glory, Lord of love;
Hearts unfold like flowers before you,
Opening to the sun above.
Melt the clouds of sin and sadness;
Drive the dark of doubt away;
Giver of eternal gladness,
Fill us with the light of day.

Reader: (Read Matthew 25:31–45.)

(Pause for silent reflection on reading.)

Prayer Response

Leader: For failing to be aware that God is with us in our lives,

All: Jesus, we ask for forgiveness.

Leader: For the times we chose not to live for God's kingdom,

All: Jesus, we ask for forgiveness.

Leader: For the times when we did not care for the needs of others,

All: Jesus, we ask for forgiveness.

Leader: For the times when we did not care for people who are hungry,

All: Jesus, we ask for forgiveness.

Leader: For the times we were not peacemakers,

All: Jesus, we ask for forgiveness.

All: (Pray the Our Father together.)

Leader: Let us exchange a sign of peace with one another.

Closing Hymn
Sing to the tune of "Joyful, Joyful!"

Jesus, Jesus please forgive us,
For the times we did not love.
We will try to be disciples,
And spread peace and joy to all.
Thank you, God, for your forgiveness
For our failings and our sins.
We are joyful for God's blessings,
Helping us to love again.

Talk with your catechist about ways you and your family can use the "Faith Alive" pages together. Work with a family member and discuss the values checklist.

In this lesson your fourth grader was reminded about the way God wants us to live and about the gift of the sacrament of Reconciliation. It is important that we help our children understand the connection between reconciliation and conversion. Conversion is a lifelong process of turning *away* from sin and turning *toward* God. Reconciliation heals us and strengthens us to continue our journey toward God. It involves both trying not to sin again and making up with those whom our sins have hurt. It might help you and your child to examine, not just actual sins, but the *values* that underlie the choices made. Do the following checklist with your child and talk about values.

Values Checklist

- ☐ It is important to me to get what I want.
- ☐ It is all right to do wrong things if no one gets hurt.
- ☐ It is important to me how my actions affect others.
- ☐ When I hurt someone, I need to say and show that I am sorry.
- ☐ If no one sees me, it is all right to steal.
- ☐ It is important to me to be at peace with my family and others.

† Family Prayer

Oh God,
you have given me ears to hear you,
 and so I answer, "Here I am;
  your instructions for me are in
   the book of the Law.
How I love to do your will, my God!
 I keep your teaching in my heart."
Based on Psalm 40:6–8

Learn by heart Faith Summary

- We sin when we freely choose to do what is wrong. We disobey God's law on purpose.

- God always forgives us when we are sorry.

- We examine our conscience to prepare for Reconciliation.

Review

Go over the *Faith Summary* together and encourage your child to learn it by heart, especially the first statement. Then help your child to complete the *Review*. The answers to numbers 1–4 appear on page 216. The response to number 5 will indicate how well your fourth grader is growing in what it means to follow Jesus. When the *Review* is completed, go over it together.

Circle T (True) or F (False).

1. When we choose to do something we know is wrong, we sin.   T   F

2. We prepare for Reconciliation by examining
how people have hurt us.   T   F

3. God always forgives us when we are sorry.   T   F

4. When we are truly sorry we promise to change.   T   F

5. How will you try harder to live as Jesus' disciple?

_____

_____

_____

_____

FAMILY SCRIPTURE MOMENT

Gather and ask: Why do we sometimes see others as our enemies? Then **Listen** to the good news that we are reconciled in Christ.

Whoever is in Christ is a new creation. . . . And all this is from God, who has reconciled us to himself through Christ and given us the ministry of reconciliation. . . . So we are ambassadors for Christ, as if God were appealing through us. We implore you on behalf of Christ, be reconciled to God. For our sake he made him to be sin who did not know sin, so that we might become the righteousness of God in him.

2 Corinthians 5:17–18, 20–21

Share what it means for you to carry on the ministry of reconciliation. Are there times when we see ourselves as enemies of or strangers to God? Why or why not?

Consider for family enrichment:

■ Paul reminds the Corinthians that they are to participate in Jesus' ministry of reconciling all people to God.

■ We help others to become friends of God by sharing our faith and by our willingness to seek and to offer forgiveness.

Reflect and **Decide** How is the ministry of reconciliation practiced in our parish and in our family? How will we participate in this ministry?

48

Jesus, may the Eucharist help us to share our lives with others.

Our Life

Special Friends: A Play

Anna: Mrs. Carr, what a great trip to the community center! It was like spending the day with my grandparents. Everyone was so friendly.

Mrs. Carr: It seems like we all enjoyed the day. How about if we take turns to share what we remember.

Mike: Mr. Ricco is a good story teller. His stories about the war made me feel I was right there with him.

Chris: Everyone really liked our sandwiches and cookies! Mrs. Beltmen told me we should get the golden apron award.

Ashley: Did you see how Mr. Drake carved a face in my apple? It looked so real I didn't want to ruin it by eating it.

Mrs. Carr: Do you remember the song all our new friends sang before we ate our lunch? Let's sing it together.

Jerome: Oh, I remember it! Mrs. Foster played it on the piano. She said it was the same tune as "She'll Be Coming 'Round the Mountain."

All: Let us show that we are grateful for God's gifts.
Let us show that we are grateful for God's gifts.
Let us praise our God in heaven.
Let us all sing our thanksgiving.
Let us show that we are grateful for God's gifts.

What have you learned from senior citizens you know?

How do you show your thanks for older people?

Sharing Life

Imagine Jesus came to share a meal with us. What would we talk to him about?

Do you think Jesus is with you when you share with others? How?

The Eucharist

Jesus Christ is with us today in a special way in the Eucharist. We celebrate the Eucharist at Mass, our greatest prayer of praise and thanks to God. The Mass is both a meal and a sacrifice. Together as a parish family, we gather as a worshiping assembly for the celebration of Mass.

At Mass we remember all that Jesus did to save us. At the Last Supper, on the night before he died, Jesus celebrated the feast of Passover with his friends.

During the meal, Jesus took bread and gave thanks to God. He gave the bread to his friends and said, "Take this all of you, and eat it: this is my body, which will be given up for you."

Then he took a cup of wine and gave thanks to God. He gave the cup to his disciples and said, "Take this, all of you, and drink from it; this is the cup of my blood, the blood of the new and everlasting covenant."

The bread and wine were now the Body and Blood of Jesus, even though they still looked and tasted like bread and wine. Jesus told his friends, "Do this in memory of me."

Jesus showed us how much he loved us by giving us this wonderful gift of himself in Holy Communion. When we celebrate the Mass, we thank God that Jesus is really with us. Jesus promised his disciples that he would never leave them. Jesus said, "I am with you always, until the end of the age" (Matthew 28:20).

The Last Supper by Phillipe de Champaigne, circa 1648

We Celebrate the Eucharist

In the Liturgy of the Word, we come together as an assembly of faith. We listen to the Bible readings to hear what God is saying to us today. We pray a psalm and proclaim our faith. We ask God to help us.

In the Liturgy of the Eucharist, we give thanks to God the Father and offer him gifts of bread and wine. Through the power of the Holy Spirit and the words and actions of the priest, our gifts become the Body and Blood of Christ.

The priest breaks the consecrated Host. This reminds us that we all receive the one Bread of Life in Holy Communion. We know that we are united with one another in Jesus Christ when we share his Body and Blood in Holy Communion. Jesus is with us. We tell him what is in our hearts.

Learn and pray together the "Holy, holy, holy" that we pray at Mass. (See page 73.)

Coming To Faith

Tell in your words what Jesus did at the Last Supper.

What can you say to Jesus the next time you receive him in Holy Communion?
Write your prayer below.

† Dear Jesus,

_____

_____

_____

_____

_____

PRACTICING FAITH

Preparing a Mass
Divide into small groups. Review the parts of the Mass. Write down the plan for your group Mass.

Theme: Ask your catechist to help you find the readings in the Lectionary for the Mass. Read them and decide together the theme of this Mass.

Introductory Rites
Hymn: Choose an opening hymn.

_____

Liturgy of the Word
Readings: Choose people to read the two readings from the Bible and the psalm response.

Old Testament reading:

   Book, Chapter, Verses

   _____

   Reader: _____

Psalm and New Testament reading:

   Psalm Response

   _____

   Book, Chapter, Verses

   _____

   Reader: _____

Prayer of the Faithful: Write several petitions to use at Mass.

_____

_____

Liturgy of the Eucharist
Presentation of Gifts: Decide who will bring up the plate or ciborium, which contains the altar breads, and the wine and water.

   Bread _____

   Wine _____

   Water _____

Concluding Rite
Hymn: Choose a hymn of thanksgiving.

_____

Talk with your catechist about ways you and your family might use the "Faith Alive" pages. As a family, you might want to make a list of people who need your prayers.

FAITH ALIVE AT HOME AND IN THE PARISH

In this lesson your fourth grader was reminded of the meaning of the Eucharist and its central importance in the lives of Catholic Christians. The Eucharist has been a central mystery of our faith from the earliest days of the Church. We read in the Acts of the Apostles that the early Christians "devoted themselves to the teaching of the apostles and to the communal life, to the breaking of the bread and to the prayers" (Acts 2:42). They also held all goods and property in common and provided for each member according to need. The sharing of the Eucharist was an extension of a life shared in mutual concern and service.

You might ask yourself:

■ *How does our family express our appreciation of the Eucharist?*

Yes, I Believe

Say the word "Amen." When you pray this word you are saying, "Yes, it is so." With a family member pray the prayer together. Decorate the frame.

† I believe that I receive the body and blood of Jesus Christ in Holy Communion.

† **Family Prayer**
Jesus, you come to us,
As Bread to feed us,
Friend to heal us,
Light to lead us.
Welcome, Jesus, welcome!

Learn by heart **Faith Summary**

- Jesus is really present in the Eucharist.

- The Eucharist is our greatest prayer of praise and thanksgiving to God.

- We share the Body and Blood of Christ in Holy Communion.

Review

Go over the *Faith Summary* together and encourage your child to learn it by heart. Then help your fourth grader complete the *Review*. The answers to numbers 1–4 appear on page 216. The response to number 5 will indicate how well your child understands what Jesus did at the Last Supper. When the *Review* is completed, go over it together.

Fill in the blanks.

Mass   Body   Blood   Word   bread   wine

1. The _____ is our greatest prayer of praise and thanksgiving to God.

2. In Holy Communion we receive the _____ and _____ of Christ.

3. In the Liturgy of the Word we listen to God's _____ .

4. In the Liturgy of the Eucharist the priest offers God gifts of

_____ and _____ .

5. In your own words tell what Jesus did at the Last Supper.

_____

_____

FAMILY SCRIPTURE MOMENT

Gather and invite family members to name a priest they know and respect very much. Ask: How have priests served us? How have we served them? Then **Listen** to this description of Jesus Christ, the High Priest.

Therefore, since we have a great high priest who has passed through the heavens, Jesus, the Son of God, let us hold fast to our confession. For we do not have a high priest who is unable to sympathize with our weaknesses, but one who has similarly been tested in every way, yet without sin. So let us confidently approach the throne of grace to receive mercy and to find grace for timely help.
Hebrews 4:14–16.

Share what we believe about Jesus being tempted as we are. What do we learn from this?

Consider for family enrichment:

■ The Letter to the Hebrews praises Jesus as our human and divine High Priest, who intercedes with God for us.

■ Through the sacrificial banquet of the Eucharist, we enter into the saving mystery of Christ's passion, death, and resurrection.

Reflect How does this image of Jesus as our High Priest encourage or challenge us?

Decide What graces will we seek when we celebrate Eucharist this week?

UNIT 1 ▪ REVIEW

Living for God's Kingdom

Jesus preached the good news of the kingdom of God. The good news is that God loves us and is always with us in our lives. Jesus showed us that we live for God's kingdom when we do his loving will.

We take responsibility for loving and caring for others. We make a decision to live a life of love, peace, and justice for all, as Jesus showed us.

The Virtues of Faith, Hope, and Love

Faith, hope, and love are great Christian virtues. A virtue is a habit of doing good.

We have faith in God. We believe and trust in God.

We have hope in God, too. We know that God will always help us, no matter what happens. We have hope because God wants us to enjoy eternal life, which lasts forever.

Love enables us to love God, ourselves, and our neighbors as ourselves.

Practicing the virtues of faith, hope, and love helps us to work together for God's kingdom.

The Church, Jesus' Community

Jesus promised his disciples that he would send them a Helper. After Jesus returned to his Father, the Holy Spirit came at Pentecost to the disciples as their Helper.

The Holy Spirit guides us and helps our Church to live as Jesus showed us. Our Church preaches, serves, worships, and cares for all people. We belong to Jesus' community by belonging to the Catholic Church.

The Beatitudes

The Beatitudes are ways of living that Jesus gave us to be truly happy. The Holy Spirit helps us to have the courage to choose to live the Beatitudes.

Review the chart on pages 32 and 33.

Living as Our Best Selves

Jesus told us that we will be judged by the way we treat one another. The Corporal and Spiritual Works of Mercy guide us in treating others as Jesus taught us. Review the charts on page 39.

When we live the Corporal and Spiritual Works of Mercy, we bring justice and mercy to all people. We live as our best selves. We help to bring about God's kingdom.

UNIT 1 ■ TEST

Circle the correct answer.

1. Jesus preached about the
  a. rosary.
  b. holy days of obligation.
  c. good news of God's kingdom.

2. Faith, hope, and love are
  a. laws of the Church.
  b. virtues.
  c. beatitudes.

3. The Holy Spirit
  a. came on Pentecost.
  b. guides and helps the Church.
  c. both of the above.

4. The Beatitudes teach us to
  a. fight with others.
  b. be truly happy.
  c. make a lot of money.

Answer these questions.

5. What is the kingdom of God?

_____

_____

6. What does it mean to live with hope?

_____

_____

7. Tell how our Church cares for people.

_____

_____

8. What are the Beatitudes?

_____

_____

9. Name one beatitude.

_____

10. How do the Works of Mercy help us to live as Jesus taught?

_____

_____

Child's name _____

Your child has just completed Unit 1. Mark and return the checklist to the catechist. It will help both you and the catechist know how to help your child's growth in faith.

_____ My child needs help with the part of the Review I have underlined.

_____ My child understands how we can build up the kingdom of God.

_____ I would like to speak with you. My phone number is _____.

(Signature) _____

8 | Living as God's People

O God, your
law is good.
It gives us
strength and
guidance.

OUR LIFE

Grandmother was going to drive the twins to the community's baseball game. "Please put your seat belts on," the twins' grandmother said. "It is the law when people ride in a car."

"That's a silly law," Brian said.

"I don't want to be strapped in. I like to move around," Marcia added.

The twins were not happy, but they did not want to be late for the game. So they did what their grandmother wanted and obeyed the law. They had only driven a few blocks when their car was hit by another car that had run a red light. The police officer said they were lucky not to be seriously injured. "Your seat belts saved your lives," he said.

What are some laws that you follow each day? Make a list together.

How does each law help us?

SHARING LIFE

Does God have rules and laws for us to follow? What are they?

Why does God give us laws to live by?

Imagine what would happen in our lives without good laws. Tell about it.

The Ten Commandments

In the Bible we read how God rescued the Israelites from slavery and made them God's own people. The Israelites had spent many years as slaves in Egypt. But God wanted them to be free.

God chose Moses to lead the Israelites out of Egypt to freedom. Once free, they came to a place called Mount Sinai. Then Moses went up the mountain, where God made a covenant, or agreement, with the people. God told Moses to tell the people, "If you hearken to my voice and keep my covenant, you shall be my special possession, dearer to me than all other people."
Based on Exodus 12:31—19:5

Then God gave Moses special commandments, or laws, that would help the people keep their covenant with God and live in peace with one another. We call them the Ten Commandments. Living the Ten Commandments would help the Israelites to remain free as God's own people.

The Ten Commandments are God's law for us today. They help us to live with true freedom as God's people. When we follow the Ten Commandments, we show that we belong to God and that we put him first in our lives.

God makes a special covenant with us at our Baptism. As Christians, we, too, are God's own people. God promises to be with us always to love and help us. We promise to obey the Ten Commandments. We promise to live as disciples of Jesus by living the Law of Love.

The **Ten Commandments** are laws given to us by God to help us live as his people.

We say yes to God's covenant by living responsibly. Doing God's loving will is our best way to live in true freedom.

The Ten Commandments are laws for living with the freedom that God wants us to have. They help us to live the Law of Love, which Jesus taught.

The Ten Commandments

1. I, the LORD, am your God, who brought you out of . . . that place of slavery. You shall not have other gods besides me.
2. You shall not take the name of the LORD, your God, in vain.
3. Remember to keep holy the sabbath day.
4. Honor your father and your mother.
5. You shall not kill.
6. You shall not commit adultery.
7. You shall not steal.
8. You shall not bear false witness against your neighbor.
9. You shall not covet your neighbor's wife.
10. You shall not covet your neighbor's house . . . nor anything else that belongs to him.

Based on Exodus 20:2–17

The LAW of LOVE

The first three commandments help us to love and honor God. The Law of Love tells us, "Love the Lord, your God, with all your heart, with all your being, with all your strength, and with all your mind."

The last seven commandments help us to love others and ourselves.

The Law of Love also tells us, "Love your neighbor as yourself."
Based on Luke 10:27

COMING TO FAITH

Make a set of cards with these key words as shown. Divide into two teams. Choose captains. The captain of each team will, in turn, choose a card and ask a member of the opposite team to tell everything he or she knows about the word. Your catechist will be the judge and rate the response: 3 (fantastic), 2 (okay), or 1 (keep working).

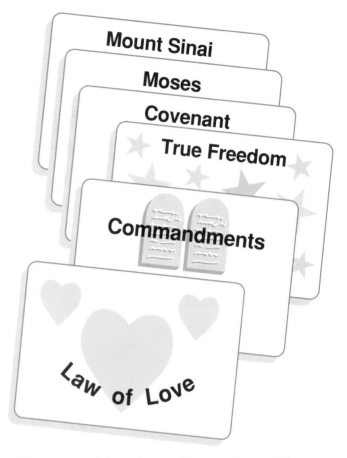

PRACTICING FAITH

God has made a covenant with us. We, on our part, have made a covenant with God to keep the commandments and live as God's people.

Work together to draw up your own "group covenant" with God for this year. Choose something special to do together to show you are God's people.

Plan your ideas here. Share them. Then write down the "group covenant." When it is completed, have someone read it aloud to the group. Then pray together the Our Father.

God,
We promise to try to

_____

_____

_____

Talk with your catechist about ways you and your family might use the "Faith Alive" pages together. Ask a family member to help you learn the Ten Commandments by heart. Pray the prayer from Psalm 19 with your catechist and friends.

In this lesson your fourth grader learned that the Ten Commandments help us to do God's loving will for us. Notice that before God gave the Israelites the first commandments, he reminded them about who set them free. God gives us the Ten Commandments to help us live in true freedom. They can also help us to grow strong, wise, and happy in our lives as Catholic Christians.

Go over the Ten Commandments with your family. Talk about why God gave them to us. Discuss the fact that for each person some commandments are harder to keep than others. Then share ways we can support one another in keeping the commandments and the Law of Love.

"Key" Promises

Read God's covenant in Exodus 34:10–11. Talk with family members about the "key" ideas that God promises in this reading. Then use a large piece of paper to cut out a key like the one below. Write on the key "We want to be God's people. We try to do his will." Invite the members of your family to sign their names as they share one "key" way they will try to do God's will. You might want to place this key in your family Bible.

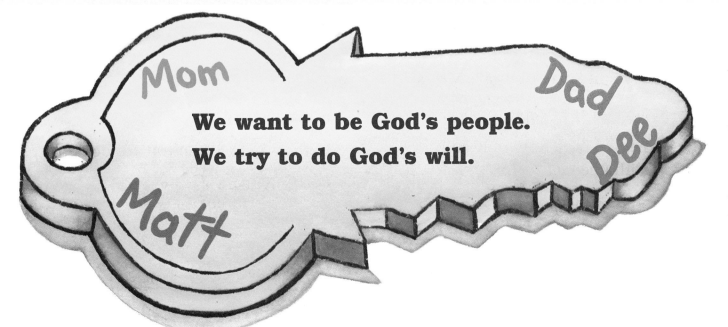

Mom

Dad

Dee

Matt

We want to be God's people.
We try to do God's will.

† Family Prayer

Pray this psalm that Jews as well as Christians pray to thank God for the Ten Commandments.

The law of the LORD is perfect,
   refreshing the soul.
The decree of the LORD is trustworthy,
   giving wisdom to the simple.
The precepts of the LORD are right,
   rejoicing the heart.
The command of the LORD is clear,
   enlightening the eye.
Psalm 19: 8–10

Learn by heart Faith Summary

- God gave Moses the Ten Commandments to give to the people.

- The Ten Commandments help us to live with true freedom as God's people.

- The Ten Commandments help us to live the Law of Love, which Jesus taught.

Review

Go over the *Faith Summary* together and encourage your child to learn it by heart, especially the second statement. Then help your fourth grader complete the *Review.* The answers to numbers 1–4 appear on page 216.

The response to number 5 will show how well your fourth grader understands that he or she made a covenant at Baptism to live as a disciple of Jesus. When the *Review* is completed, go over it together.

Circle the letter beside the correct answer.

1. God told Moses to

   a. make a covenant with the Egyptians.

   b. fight the Egyptians.

   c. lead the Israelites to freedom.

2. On Mount Sinai, God gave Moses

   a. laws for the people to obey.

   b. help to live responsibly and with freedom.

   c. both of the above

3. The Ten Commandments help us

   a. never to have bad times.

   b. to live Jesus' Law of Love.

   c. seem to be better than others.

4. Doing God's will is

   a. always easy.

   b. the way to live in true freedom.

   c. like living in slavery.

5. What will you do to live your Baptism covenant with God?

_____

FAMILY SCRIPTURE MOMENT

Gather and invite each person to imagine: "If I were completely free, I would...." Then **Listen** to Saint Paul's call to true freedom.

For you were called for freedom, brothers. But do not use this freedom as an opportunity for the flesh; rather, serve one another through love. For the whole law is fulfilled in one statement, namely, "You shall love your neighbor as yourself." But if you go on biting and devouring one another, beware that you are not consumed by one another. I say then: live by the Spirit....

Galatians 5:13–16

Share what each family member heard in this reading, especially what seemed most important.

Consider for family enrichment:

■ Paul's Letter to the Galatians is a powerful declaration of Christian freedom. When we are guided by the Spirit, love becomes the only law that binds us.

■ If we allow ourselves to be ruled by our bodily desires or negative emotions, we are no longer free. Living God's law sets us free.

Reflect and **Decide** Are there ways in which we have harmed or hurt one another? As a family, how will we let the Holy Spirit direct our lives this week?

9 Living as Free People

Junk food/Healthy food ?

Study/Cheat ?

?Chores/T.V. ?

Our Life

Our lives are full of decisions and choices to be made. Some are so simple that they hardly need too much attention. For example, it does not require much decision making to choose to wear shoes or sneakers to school.

We need to think through other decisions more carefully. This is because some decisions we make may not be good for us. For example: If I am offered a cigarette and choose to smoke it, this decision will affect my health.

Take a few minutes to write on a small piece of paper an important choice someone your age might have to make. Fold your paper and put all the papers in a box.

Sharing Life

One by one, take a paper from the box. Read the "choice" to the group and share what you think the responsible decision should be.

What things do we think about when making a good decision?

Talk together and share your ideas.

Making Choices

God has given us a free will. This means we can choose between right and wrong. We are responsible for saying yes or no to God.

God created us free to think, to choose, and to love. We are free to be faithful to God and to live according to his loving will for us. But people do not always choose to do God's will.

Some choices are easy; others are difficult. They are difficult because it often seems easier to do the wrong thing. Sometimes others—even young people our own age—will make fun of us for doing the right thing.

Sinning by What We Do

Jesus came to show us how to choose to love God, others, and ourselves. But sometimes we choose to turn away from God. We sin. Sin is freely choosing to do what we know is wrong. When we sin, we disobey God's law on purpose.

Some people think that when they do the wrong thing by mistake, they have sinned. Everyone makes mistakes. For example, we often say or do something that we did not intend. Mistakes are not sins.

Temptations also are not sins. We may feel like stealing something. But if we choose not to steal, we have not given in to the temptation. We have not sinned.

The Catholic Church teaches us that we can sin in thought, word, or action. Some sins are so serious that by doing them we turn completely away from God's love. We call them mortal sins.

A sin is mortal when:

• what we do is very seriously wrong;

• we know that it is very wrong and that God forbids it;

• we freely choose to do it.

Some sins are less serious. We call them venial sins. We do not turn away completely from God's love but still hurt ourselves or others. We freely choose to be selfish.

All sins are personal choices. But sometimes whole groups of people can sin and hurt other people. We call this "social sin." When a group treats other people unjustly because of the color of their skin, or their age, or sex, or religion, it is a social sin.

Sin is never just between God and one person. Sin hurts us all. When we sin, we do not show love for God and his family.

Sin is freely choosing to do what we know is wrong. When we sin, we disobey God's law on purpose.

Sinning by What We Do Not Do

We can also sin by what we do *not* do, as well as by what we choose to do. If someone is badly hurt or starving, and we choose not to give help, we may sin. By standing by and doing nothing, we are choosing not to love as God commanded.

If we want to be forgiven for any sin, we must be sorry for it. If we have hurt someone by our sin, we must try to make it up to that person. We must try to get rid of all forms of sin in our lives and in our society.

God will always forgive us, no matter what we do, if we are truly sorry and try not to sin again. Ask the Holy Spirit to guide you and give you the courage always to make right choices.

COMING TO FAITH

Are the people in the following situations making choices in keeping with God's will? Tell what you would say to them.

To belong to the "in" group at school Natalie has to join them in stealing from a store.

Your neighbors do not speak to the new family that has just moved in. They come from another country. What would you say to the new family? to your neighbors?

PRACTICING FAITH

Gather in a prayer circle. Imagine that Jesus is in the center of the circle. Be as still as you can and breathe silently in and out. Think of a difficult choice you have to make or might have to make. One by one stretch your arms out to the center. Imagine your hands are holding your choice. When everyone's arms are stretched out, pray together:

† Jesus, here are our choices. Help us to make decisions that are pleasing to you and helpful to us. We know that you will never leave us to face our difficulties alone. Amen.

Talk with your catechist about ways you and your family can use the "Faith Alive" pages together. Pray the prayer for forgiveness with your catechist and friends.

In this lesson your fourth grader learned that to live in freedom, we must avoid sin. He or she learned that all sin is a personal choice. Very serious sin is called mortal sin. Less serious sin is called venial sin. Sometimes we may even sin as a group of people or as a society. This is called social sin. We can always make good moral choices. Such choices may be difficult for young children. As adults we also know how difficult it can be to do God's will and to avoid sin. Indeed, we must examine our own consciences often if we expect our children to do the same.

Making Choices

Talk with your son or daughter about the difficult choices he or she has to make regularly. Then review the checklist below. Have your fourth grader put a check next to each step after you have discussed it together. (Save this page to use with page 163.)

Checklist for Making Choices

___ Take time to think about what I am about to do.

___ Ask the Holy Spirit to guide me and give me the courage to make the right choice.

___ Look at all the possible choices.

___ See which choices will show that I love God and others.

___ Say no to the choices that will hurt me or others.

___ Go to others for help when I need advice or when it is hard to do the right thing.

___ Choose to do the right thing.

† Prayer for Forgiveness

I confess to almighty God,
and to you, my brothers and sisters,
that I have sinned through my own fault
in my thoughts and in my words,
in what I have done,
and in what I have failed to do;
and I ask blessed Mary, ever virgin,
all the angels and saints,
and you, my brothers and sisters,
to pray for me to the Lord our God.

Learn by heart ## Faith Summary

● We can sin in thought, word, or action.

● Very serious sins are called mortal sins; less serious sins are called venial sins.

● A sin is mortal when what we do is very seriously wrong; we know that it is very wrong and that God forbids it; we freely choose to do it.

Go over the *Faith Summary* together and encourage your child to learn it by heart. Then help your fourth grader complete the *Review*. The answers to numbers 1–4 appear on page 216. The response to number 5 will show whether your fourth grader understands how to make good choices. When the *Review* is completed, go over it together.

Circle the letter beside the correct answer.

1. Sin is

   a. feeling like doing something wrong.

   b. doing something wrong by mistake.

   c. disobeying God's law on purpose.

2. Mortal sin is a very serious sin by which

   a. we turn from God's love completely.

   b. we are tempted to turn from God.

   c. we do something wrong by mistake.

3. Venial sin is a less serious sin which

   a. hurts ourselves or others.

   b. ends our friendship with God.

   c. needs no forgiveness.

4. We can sin by

   a. loving one another.

   b. caring for others.

   c. choosing not to love.

5. Tell what you will do to make the right choices this week.

FAMILY SCRIPTURE MOMENT

Gather and ask: What feelings do we experience when we see people on TV or in movies doing "things that belong to darkness"? What do we do about those feelings? Then **Listen** to a message of light.

So be imitators of God, as beloved children. . . . For you were once darkness, but now you are light in the Lord. Live as children of light, for light produces every kind of goodness and righteousness and truth. Try to learn what is pleasing to the Lord. Take no part in the fruitless works of darkness; rather expose them. . . .

Ephesians 5:1, 8–11

Share what it would mean for us to "live in the light."

Consider for family enrichment:

■ Paul emphasizes that Christians can freely choose to avoid living in the darkness of sin. By choosing the light of Christ, they draw others toward God.

■ Because we can be tempted to do "worthless things," we have to make a daily effort to live in the light and always ask God's help.

Reflect and **Decide** Who or what helps us to stay in the light? Pray: Jesus, our Lord and our brother, may our example shine like a candle, guiding others.

10 God Is First in Our Lives
The First Commandment

God, we praise you! We give you glory! We put you first in our lives.

OUR LIFE

The April weather was still unpredictable when Marty and his friend Steve decided to climb in the Rocky Mountains. Both young men were experienced climbers and moved easily up the face of the cliff.

They were almost to the top when clouds rolled in and the temperature dropped steadily. As Marty was swinging to a new foothold, his rope suddenly snapped. He fell ten feet to a ledge. Steve yelled that he would go for help. The injured Marty curled up on the ledge as snow fell and a cold wind lowered his body temperature. "I thought I was going to die there," he said. "I prayed and tried to stay awake."

Then morning came clear and cold. "The sun came up like fire," Marty recalls. "Even before I heard the shouts of the rescuers, I felt full of wonder and hope. I knew I was in God's hands."

When have you felt that God was really with you? Tell about it.

SHARING LIFE

What do you think it means to put God first in your life? What are some reasons for doing this? Share your thoughts as a group.

69

The First Commandment

The Israelites trusted in God because they knew they were God's people. They had a covenant with God and knew how much he loved them. Obeying God's commandments was the way they showed they were keeping their covenant with God.

The first commandment that Moses gave them was "I, the LORD, am your God, who brought you out of . . . that place of slavery. You shall not have other gods besides me" (Exodus 20:2–3).

This commandment was very important to the Israelites. They had been slaves of the Egyptians, but God rescued them from slavery and set them free. To remain free as God's people, the Israelites had to put God first in their lives.

When something in our life becomes more important than God, we are not free. We become slaves to it.

The Israelites put God first in their lives in many ways. They worshiped God in the Temple of Jerusalem. They studied the commandments in their synagogues. What is most important, they put God first in their lives by trying to do his will—living with justice, peace, and love.

Sometimes the Israelites, like people today, found it hard to put God first in their lives. They discovered it was the only way they could live in true freedom.

The first commandment tells us to keep God first in our lives, even when that is difficult.

Here is a bible story showing that even Jesus was tempted not to obey the first commandment.

Jesus was led by the Holy Spirit into the desert. Jesus stayed there a long time. At the end of his stay in the desert, he was very hungry.

> A **covenant** is a special agreement made between God and people.

Then the devil showed Jesus all the kingdoms of the world. The devil told him "I shall give to you all this power and their glory; . . . if you worship me."

Jesus answered, "It is written:
'You shall worship the Lord, your God, and him alone shall you serve.'"

Then the devil took Jesus to Jerusalem and stood him on the highest point of the Temple. He said to Jesus, "If you are the Son of God, throw yourself down from here. . . ."

Jesus answered, "It also says, 'You shall not put the Lord, your God, to the test.'"
Based on Luke 4:1–12

Jesus did not give in to any of the devil's temptations. Jesus always put God first in his life. He helps us to do the same.

Putting God First

Today some people are tempted to make "false gods" out of food, clothes, being famous, possessions—even other people. We may be tempted to think that something is more important than God.

Living by the first commandment means that we put all our faith in God and choose to keep him first in our lives. When God is most important in our lives, we live in freedom and work to bring about his kingdom, or reign, of justice and peace for all.

It was then that Jesus was tempted by the devil. The devil said to him, "If you are the Son of God, command this stone to become bread."

Jesus answered him, "It is written, 'One does not live by bread alone.'"

COMING TO FAITH

Create an ending to these stories to show how each person chooses to live the first commandment.

Angie has a very large paper route and earns her own money. The paper route takes all her free time after school. She has no time to do her homework or to play with her friends. Her family wants her to give up some of her paper route. Angie does not want to do this. She likes the money she makes too much.

Matt is a poor loser. He always wants to be the winner. If someone else wins, he gets very angry. When asked what he wants to be when he grows up, Matt says he wants to be his own boss. "The most important thing," he says, "is looking out for number one—me."

Imagine that you have been asked to give a talk to the third grade. What suggestions would you give them about putting God first in their lives?

PRACTICING FAITH

Plan your ideas for a poster to show how you will try to live the first commandment this week. Then share these ideas and create a group poster titled "God Comes First." You might want to display it in your parish church.

Close by sharing a prayer of petition. Each one prays:

† Dear God, help us to put you first in our lives by

_____

_____

_____

Talk with your catechist about ways you and your family might use the "Faith Alive" pages. See if you can learn the first two *Faith Summary* statements by heart. Pray the Prayer of Praise with your catechist and friends.

72

FAITH ALIVE AT HOME AND IN THE PARISH

In this lesson your fourth grader learned that the first commandment tells us to put God first in our lives. Putting God first in one's life is always a challenge. With many parents holding down two jobs, caring for an aging parent, or facing serious family illness, it is no wonder people can lose their focus in life. Yet the most ancient roots of our faith tell us that it is not only a law but very wise to put God first. This helps us to keep things in perspective. Remember, too, that God is always present to us, reaching out in love to sustain and strengthen us.

You might ask yourself:

■ *What example of putting God first in my life do I give my fourth grader?*

■ *How will I do this in the coming week?*

Putting God First

To help your fourth grader better understand and follow the first commandment, complete the following activity together. Then talk about how the person pictured is putting God first.

Find or draw a picture of someone who is putting God first.

† Prayer of Praise

Pray this prayer that we say at Mass:

Holy, holy, holy Lord, God of power and might, heaven and earth are full of your glory.

Hosanna in the highest.

Blessed is he who comes in the name of the Lord.

Hosanna in the highest.

Learn by heart Faith Summary

- The first commandment is "I, the LORD, am your God, who brought you out of . . . that place of slavery. You shall not have other gods besides me."

- Jesus taught us to put God first in our lives.

- When we live the first commandment, we live in true freedom.

Review

Go over the *Faith Summary* together and encourage your child to learn it by heart, especially the first statement. Then help your fourth grader complete the *Review*. The answers to numbers 1–4 appear on page 216. Number 5 encourages your fourth grader to grow in the practice of putting God first in life, particularly in weekly worship. When the *Review* is completed, go over it together.

Match the columns.

A	B
1. Jesus was tempted by	_____ we put God first
2. The first commandment is	_____ the kingdom, or reign, of God
3. When God is most important in our lives, we help to bring about	_____ the devil
4. To obey the first commandment	_____ You shall not have other gods besides me

5. Tell how and why you will worship God this week.

_____

_____

_____

FAMILY SCRIPTURE MOMENT

Gather and invite each person to draw or describe a "warning" sign against an idol (something one is tempted to make more important than God). Ask: What are some of the things idols require of us? Then **Listen** to a warning from Saint Paul about idols.

So about the eating of meat sacrificed to idols: we know that. . . "there is no God but one."
. . . one God, the Father,
    from whom all things are and for whom
        we exist,
  and one Lord, Jesus Christ,
    through whom all things are and through
        whom we exist.
But not all have this knowledge.
1 Corinthians 8:4, 6–7

Share what each one thinks are some of the most dangerous idols in our society today.

Consider for family enrichment:

■ In this letter, Paul wants the Christians of Corinth to understand that, even if their food has been sacrificed to pagan gods before it reached them, it cannot harm them. The "gods" are not real.

■ Idols cannot harm us if we say no to them and if we remember to keep God at the center of our lives.

Reflect and **Decide** Think of what the most dangerous idol is for our family, the one most tempting. Then ask: How can we best reject it and show that our family belongs to the one true God?

74

11 God's Name Is Holy
The Second Commandment

Lamb of God, you take away the sin of the world. Give us peace.

OUR LIFE

A young boy named Corey was in a very serious accident. He was rushed to the hospital in a coma. The doctors were worried about him because he showed no signs of coming out of the coma. The family took turns staying with Corey and talking quietly to him.

One day after visiting the hospital's chapel, Corey's father went to his son's room. He stood at the foot of the bed and called his son's name in a loud voice, "Corey!" At that moment, Corey's eyes slowly opened. He smiled at his father.

What do you learn from this story?

What does a person's name really stand for?

How do I show respect for a person's name?

SHARING LIFE

Talk together about the names you have for God.

What are some things you think of when you hear God's name—for example, love?

Why do you think we should show respect for God's name?

The Second Commandment

The people of Israel believed that respecting a person's name was a way of showing respect for that person. They showed special respect for God's name.

God had said, "I am who am. . . ."
"This is my name forever."
Based on Exodus 3:14–15

The words "I am who am" make up the Hebrew word *Yahweh*. Yahweh was the name that the Israelites called God.

The second commandment of God is "You shall not take the name of the LORD, your God, in vain" (Exodus 20:7). The people of Israel had such great respect for God's name that they did not speak his name out loud.

Jesus taught his disciples to pray to God, saying, "Our Father, who art in heaven, hallowed be thy name." The word *hallowed* means holy and worthy of praise. Jesus was telling the disciples that God's name is truly holy. We must use God's name with great respect and praise him.

Jesus also respected holy places that honored God. One time, Jesus went to the Temple in Jerusalem to pray. Some people were using the Temple as a place to buy and sell things.

Jesus chased them out of the Temple. He said, "It is written:
'My house shall be
a house of prayer,'
but you are making it
a den of thieves."
Based on Matthew 21:12–13

Keeping God's Name Holy

The second commandment reminds us that God's name is holy. God's name and all places that honor God must always be treated with honor and respect. When we do this, we live the second commandment.

We must also show respect for the holy name of Jesus. Saint Paul tells us that God gave Jesus the name that is greater than any other name. And so, everyone must honor the name of Jesus and say that "Jesus Christ is Lord."

Based on Philippians 2:9–11

Sometimes people use God's name or Jesus' name when they are angry. They use God's name to curse, or wish bad things, on someone. To use God's name or Jesus' name in vain is wrong and is a sin.

Sometimes we are asked to swear on God's name that something is true. Swearing is calling on God to be our witness.

Witnesses in court swear, or call on God, to witness that they are telling the truth. Swearing is only for serious occasions such as this. It is a very serious sin to swear on God's name and then to tell lies.

We must always use God's holy name and the holy name of Jesus Christ with love and great respect.

We are disrespectful to God's name and Jesus' name when we use them in vain. We take God's name in vain when we use it for no reason other than to express our anger or to "show off."

Coming to Faith

How should we live the second commandment? Tell what you would say about Leo and Janine.

Leo says that all his friends swear and curse, using God's name. Leo does not want to be different from the others so he swears too.

Janine is your very good friend. You really like her. But Janine often uses the name of Jesus in a disrespectful way. She says she just does it to be funny.

Practicing Faith

We have many names that describe God. Each one is a word of praise for God's goodness and greatness. Think of your favorite name for God. Write it here.

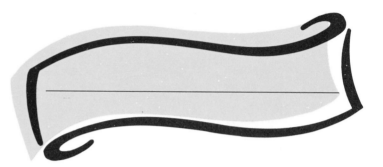

Gather with your friends in a circle. Take turns sharing your favorite names for God. Tell why they are your favorites. Then pray:

† O God, we love your name. (Each one, in turn, softly calls aloud the name of God he or she chose.) We will honor your name always. Amen.

Sing together:

Holy God, we praise thy name;
Lord of all, we bow before thee;
All on earth thy scepter claim.
All in heaven above adore thee;
Infinite, thy vast domain,
Everlasting is thy reign.
Infinite, thy vast domain,
Everlasting is thy reign.

Talk with your catechist about ways you and your family can use the "Faith Alive" pages together. You might especially want to do the activity on Jesus' holy name. Then pray the *Abba* prayer with your catechist and friends.

FAITH ALIVE AT HOME AND IN THE PARISH

In this lesson your fourth grader has learned about the second commandment and about honoring God's name, the holy name of Jesus, and holy places. Showing reverence for God's holy name is an essential expression of our Christian faith. Likewise, when we take an oath, we call on God to be our witness. This is a sacred use of his name and must never be done in vain.

Does your child see that the holy names of God and Jesus and holy places are honored by all in your family? Talk to your family about the importance of setting a good example of reverence for God's name and the name of Jesus.

Jesus' Name

As a family read Matthew 1:21 to learn that Jesus' name means "God saves"—we know that God has saved us from our sins through Jesus. Now have your fourth grader decorate the following activity.

Jesus' name means GOD SAVES

† Praying to God as Abba

Jesus called God "Abba." This term of endearment means "Father," telling us that God is like a loving parent. Gather as a family in some quiet place. Remind everyone that God is present. Then invite each family member to say the word *Abba* over and over slowly and talk to God in his or her own words.

Learn by heart Faith Summary

- The second commandment is "You shall not take the name of the LORD, your God, in vain."

- We live the second commandment by respecting God's name, the name of Jesus, and holy places.

- Cursing is wishing evil on someone. Swearing is calling on God to be our witness that we are telling the truth.

Review

Go over the *Faith Summary* together and help your child to learn it by heart, especially the first statement. Then help your child complete the *Review.* The answers to numbers 1–4 appear on page 216. The response to number 5 will help you to see how well your fourth grader is trying to honor God's name and sacred places. When the *Review* is completed, go over it together.

Answer these questions.

1. What does the second commandment ask us to do?

_____

_____

2. What is swearing?

_____

_____

3. Who is the one called I AM?

_____

_____

4. Why is cursing a sin?

_____

_____

5. This week, how will you honor God's holy name?

_____

_____

_____

FAMILY SCRIPTURE MOMENT

Gather and invite family members to tell what their given names mean to them. Ask: How do we show—or fail to show—respect for one another's names? Then **Listen** as Paul praises the greatest name of all.

> He humbled himself,
> becoming obedient to death,
>   even death on a cross.
> Because of this, God greatly exalted him
>   and bestowed on him the name
>   that is above every name,
>   that at the name of Jesus
>   every knee should bend,
> of those in heaven and on earth and under the earth,
>   and every tongue confess that
> Jesus Christ is Lord.

Philippians 2:8–11

Share some ways to show respect for the holy name of Jesus.

Consider for family enrichment:

▪ This letter from Paul in prison is an enthusiastic song of praise for Jesus, whose name should move all living beings to worship and praise.

▪ We honor the name of Jesus, which means "God saves," by using it only to share our faith and in prayer.

Reflect and **Decide** How might our parish encourage respect for the holy name of Jesus? How will we pursue this goal?

12 We Worship God
The Third Commandment

Our Life

It was late Friday afternoon. Rebecca was going home from school with her best friend, Nora. When they got there, Rebecca's mother had already prepared the evening meal and was getting ready to light the special Sabbath candles. Rebecca and her family are Jews and practice the Jewish religion.

Nora said to Rebecca, "I thought that the Jewish Sabbath was on Saturday."

"Our Jewish Sabbath begins on Friday night," said Rebecca. "The rabbi told us that in the Bible people describe each day as beginning the evening before. Our Sabbath day begins at sunset on Friday and ends at sunset on Saturday."

Nora explained, "The Christian Sabbath is on Sunday to remember the day Jesus rose from the dead."

Tell some of the things that you and your family do to make Sunday special.

Sharing Life

Do you think it is important to keep Sunday a holy day? Why or why not?

Share together how Christians can grow in keeping our Sabbath holy.

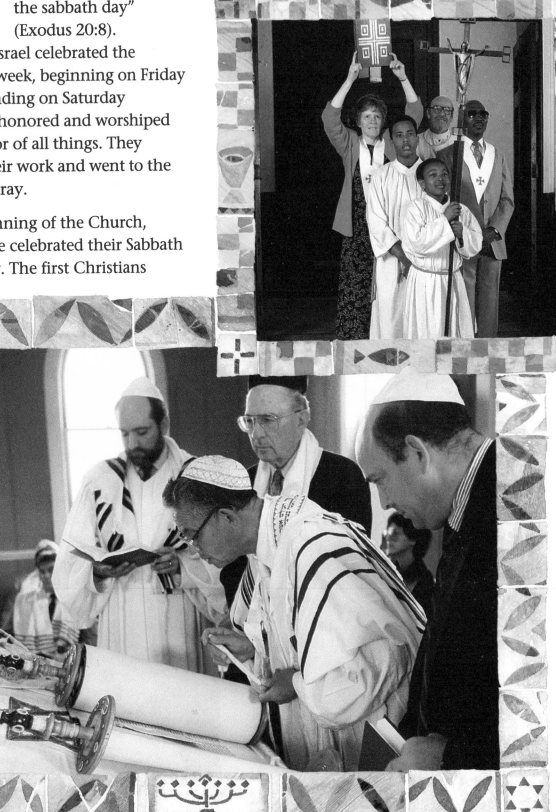

OUR CATHOLIC FAITH

The Third Commandment

The third commandment that God gave Moses was "Remember to keep holy the sabbath day" (Exodus 20:8).

The people of Israel celebrated the Sabbath every week, beginning on Friday evening and ending on Saturday evening. They honored and worshiped God, the creator of all things. They rested from their work and went to the synagogue to pray.

From the beginning of the Church, Christians have celebrated their Sabbath day on Sunday. The first Christians remembered that Jesus rose from the dead on Easter Sunday. Sunday became known as the Lord's special day and our Christian Sabbath.

Today Christians celebrate Sunday by setting aside time to rest, to turn to God, and to worship God as a community. Catholics come together with our parish community to celebrate the Mass. We listen to the word of God and receive Jesus in Holy Communion. We leave Mass ready to serve God by serving others.

Living the Commandment

The Catholic Church teaches that attending Mass on Sunday or on Saturday evening is a serious obligation. This means that Catholics must take part in the Mass unless there is a very good reason for missing, such as serious sickness.

We may anticipate, or look ahead, to Sunday Mass by celebrating it on Saturday evening. When it is not possible for us to go to Mass, we should try to read the Scriptures and say our prayers at home.

The Church also teaches that on Sundays we must try to rest, especially from unnecessary work. We keep the Sabbath holy by taking time to take care of our minds and bodies. We also try to spend fun time with our family and friends.

We need to think about doing God's will by loving God and our neighbor better during the coming week. We also think of what it means to live for God's kingdom. In these ways we live the third commandment, "Remember to keep holy the sabbath day."

The word **Sabbath** comes from a Jewish word that means "rest."

There are also other days that we try to keep holy. These are called holy days of obligation. These days remind us to celebrate some event in the life of Jesus Christ, the Blessed Virgin Mary, or the other saints.

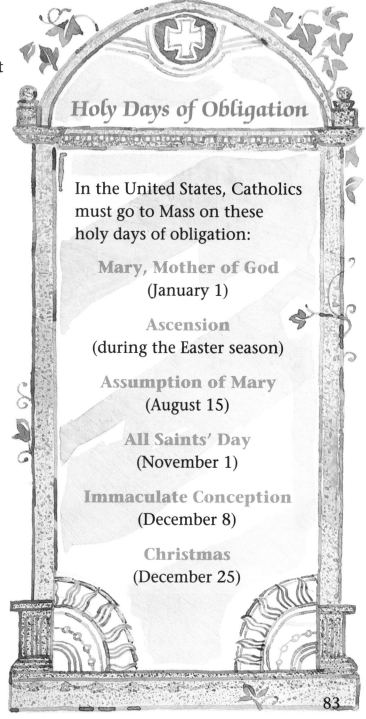

Holy Days of Obligation

In the United States, Catholics must go to Mass on these holy days of obligation:

Mary, Mother of God
(January 1)

Ascension
(during the Easter season)

Assumption of Mary
(August 15)

All Saints' Day
(November 1)

Immaculate Conception
(December 8)

Christmas
(December 25)

COMING TO FAITH

Change each story to show the third commandment being lived.

Kathy goes to Sunday Mass because her mother makes her go. All through Mass, Kathy wishes that she were somewhere else. She never pays attention or joins in the Mass.

George always waits until Sunday to do his homework. He says that he does not have time to go to Mass, because he must spend all day Sunday doing his book reports and other assignments.

Imagine that you have a friend who belongs to another religion, or has no religion at all. Explain to your friend why Catholics celebrate Mass on Sunday. What would you say?

Are you glad we have Sunday as a day to rest and to celebrate our faith? Why or why not?

PRACTICING FAITH

How will you make Sunday a holy day for you?

Finish these sentences by drawing or writing what you will try to do.

I will take time off for fun and recreation by...

I will worship God by...

I will take time to be with my friends and family by...

Talk with your catechist about ways you and your family might use the "Faith Alive" pages. Go over the checklist with a family member and pray the Family Prayer together.

FAITH ALIVE AT HOME AND IN THE PARISH

In this lesson your fourth grader learned the third commandment and why Christians keep Sunday as their Sabbath day. On Sunday we remember and celebrate the resurrection of Jesus. Each Sunday should be a special time of rest, fun, and prayer. The word *Sabbath* literally means "rest." Keeping the Sabbath holy and as a day of rest is one of the richest aspects of our faith tradition. In our busy modern world, we are once again challenged to learn what it means to keep the Sabbath day holy.

Help your fourth grader develop the habit of participating in the celebration of Mass each Sunday or Saturday evening. Make this celebration a family event. Assist your child to grow in an appreciation of Sunday Mass as that most important time each week when we worship and praise God in the community of Christian faith. This is why the Church considers weekly Mass a serious obligation.

Help your fourth grader to enjoy taking part in the Mass. Make sure he or she uses the missalette or another Mass book. Offer to bring the gifts to the altar during Mass as a family.

Preparing to Celebrate

Check what you will do as a family to prepare to celebrate Mass this weekend. Then add your own ideas.

Getting Ready for Mass

☐ Decide which Mass you will attend as a family.

☐ Think about the things you each want to talk to Jesus about.

☐ Get everyone in the family to be enthusiastic about the celebration of Mass.

☐ _____

† Family Prayer

After Mass, do something together as a family that allows you to enjoy one another's company. Then pray:

Our loving God, you have given us our Sabbath day for worship and rest. Recreate a happy heart in us, O God, as we come together in your name. Amen.

Learn by heart Faith Summary

- The third commandment is "Remember to keep holy the sabbath day."

- Christians celebrate their Sabbath on Sunday. We remember that Jesus rose from the dead on Easter Sunday.

- Catholics must take part in the Mass on Sunday or on Saturday evening and on all holy days of obligation.

Go over the *Faith Summary* together and encourage your child to learn it by heart, especially the first statement. Then help your child complete the *Review*. The answers to numbers 1–4 appear on page 216. The response to number 5 will help you to see how well your fourth grader is growing in making Sunday a truly holy day. When the *Review* is completed, go over it together.

Cross out the word or words that are incorrect.

1. The third commandment asks us to keep holy the Sabbath by (taking part in Mass, staying in bed all day).

2. On the Sabbath we try to (work harder, rest from unnecessary work).

3. On Sunday, Christians remember (the first Christmas, the first Easter).

4. Catholics must celebrate Mass on Sundays and (feast days, holy days of obligation).

5. How will you make this Sunday a truly holy day?

_____

_____

_____

FAMILY SCRIPTURE MOMENT

Gather and talk about the ways family members prepare to receive Holy Communion. Then **Listen** to Paul's message about the Lord's Supper.

For as often as you eat this bread and drink the cup, you proclaim the death of the Lord until he comes. Therefore, whoever eats the bread or drinks the cup of the Lord unworthily will have to answer for the body and blood of the Lord. A person should examine himself, and so eat the bread and drink the cup. For anyone who eats and drinks without discerning the body, eats and drinks judgment on himself.

1 Corinthians 11:26–29

Share Ask: What should we examine about our lives before we receive Jesus in Holy Communion?

Consider for family enrichment:

■ Paul was correcting those Christians who had separated themselves from the poor at the Eucharist and were not prepared to join in the celebration.

■ We cannot exclude others from our hearts if we want to receive Jesus worthily in Holy Communion. We must be ready to reach out especially to the poor and needy.

Reflect and **Decide** How are we as a family invited to grow in living the Eucharist, which we receive at Mass?

13   Celebrating Advent

Our Life

The town of Nazareth was coming awake after a long, peaceful night. Women began to fill their jars with water from the village well. One of the women was Mary.

Mary had a secret that she kept inside her heart. The angel Gabriel had come to her from God and had asked her to be the mother of God's Son.

Mary remembered the angel's words: "The child to be born will be called holy, the Son of God."

Quietly, Mary repeated the answer she had given to the angel: "I am the handmaid of the Lord. May it be done to me according to your word."

Mary had to get ready. She decided to visit her cousin Elizabeth. The angel had told Mary that Elizabeth was also about to have a baby. Mary made the long, difficult journey to visit and help her cousin, who was much older than Mary.

Mary stayed for about three months, until Elizabeth's son, John, was born. Then Mary went back home to wait for her own baby to be born.
Based on Luke 1:26–39, 56

What do you think Mary did during those months of waiting for Jesus to be born?

Have you ever waited for a younger sister or brother or cousin to be born? What did your family do to get ready?

Sharing Life

How do you feel as you wait to celebrate Jesus' birth on Christmas?

What are some of the best ways to get ready for Christmas?

87

Our Catholic Faith

A Time to Prepare

Advent is the season in which we prepare for the Lord's coming as Mary did. We prepare for the celebration of Jesus' birth at Christmas. We also remember with Mary that Jesus will come again at the end of time.

To get ready for the coming of Jesus, here are some things you might do:

- Help out at home. For example, take care of a younger child, set the table, wash the dishes, take out the garbage.

- Be extra kind to someone. For example, do something special for a tired parent, cheer up a lonely person, include someone in your group who is usually left out.

We remember that Mary prepared for Jesus' birth. We can ask Mary to help us to prepare for Christmas by remembering other people's needs, as she did.

Advent Prayers

After Elizabeth greeted Mary, Mary said a beautiful prayer of praise to God. We call it the Magnificat. Part of this prayer can be found on this page. Maybe you would like to pray it during Advent.

During Advent, we can also pray the Angelus. *Angelus* is a Latin word that means "angel." The Angelus prayer helps us to remember the time when the angel came to Mary. We remember that Mary said yes and became the mother of God's own Son.

Try to learn the Angelus by heart. You will find it on text page 90.

The Magnificat

My soul proclaims the
    greatness of the Lord;
my spirit rejoices in
    God my savior.
For he has looked upon his
    handmaid's lowliness;
behold, from now on will
    all ages call me blessed.
The Mighty One
    has done great things
    for me,
and holy is his name.
His mercy is from
    age to age
    to those who fear him.

Luke 1:46–50

Spend this Advent with Mary. Try to look at your world as she would. What might Mary do if she were living now in your family or in your neighborhood?

What will you do to prepare with Mary to celebrate Jesus' coming? Write it here.

_____

_____

Practicing Faith

We Honor Mary
An Advent Prayer Service

Opening Hymn: Hail Mary

Leader: We come together to give honor to Mary, the mother of Jesus and our mother, too. We remember how Mary said yes and became the mother of God's Son. We ask Mary to help us to be like her as we prepare to celebrate Christmas. Let us pray the Angelus together.

Side 1: The angel of the Lord declared to Mary,

Side 2: and she conceived by the Holy Spirit.

All: Hail Mary. . . .(Pray the Hail Mary together.)

Side 1: Behold the handmaid of the Lord,

Side 2: be it done to me according to your word.

All: Hail Mary. . . .

Side 1: And the Word was made flesh

Side 2: and dwelled among us.

All: Hail Mary. . . .

Side 1: Pray for us, O Holy Mother of God,

Side 2: that we may be made worthy of the promises of Christ.

Leader: Let us pray.

All: Pour forth, we beseech you, O Lord, your grace into our hearts that we to whom the incarnation of Christ your Son was made known by the message of an angel may, by his passion and death, be brought to the glory of his resurrection, through the same Christ our Lord. Amen.

Closing Hymn

Sing to the tune of "Clementine."

Mother Mary, Blessed Mother,
We all pray to you each day.
Please help us to get ready
for your Son on Christmas day.

FAITH ALIVE AT HOME AND IN THE PARISH

In this lesson Advent was presented as a time to prepare for Christmas by remembering the needs of others. The word Advent comes from the Latin verb *advenire,* which means "to come." During Advent we remember and prepare to celebrate the coming of Jesus Christ.

The Advent Gospels proclaim the final coming of Jesus Christ in glory at the end of time. In the Christian life, the best way to prepare for the end of time is by living our faith now as disciples of Jesus. This is why the Advent gospel readings emphasize the message of John the Baptist to prepare the way of the Lord in our lives and in our hearts. In this way we will also be ready to celebrate the birth of Jesus.

Encourage your fourth grader to prepare to celebrate Jesus' birth by choosing some concrete ways of helping others.

Advent Customs

If you have not already done this, you might want to begin an Advent custom for your family such as an Advent wreath, candles in the window, an Advent calendar, or a Christmas crib.

An Advent Prayer Clock

1. Cut out two large circles from heavy paper. Divide one circle into four quarters. On each of the quarters put part of the Angelus.

2. Cut a one-quarter wedge from the second circle. Color the rest of the circle purple.

3. Join the two circles with a brad.

Each week of Advent, move the top circle so a new part of the prayer can be seen. Pray the prayer with your family during Advent.

Learn by heart **Faith Summary**

- Mary prepared for Jesus by helping others.

- We prepare for Christmas by remembering the needs of others.

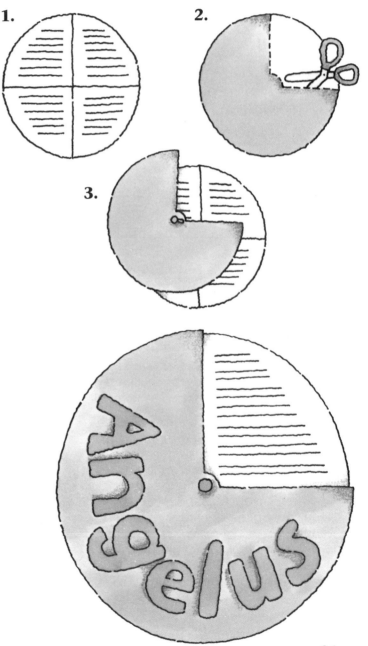

91

Review

Go over the *Faith Summary* together and encourage your child to learn it by heart. Then help your fourth grader complete the *Review*.

The answers to numbers 1–4 appear on page 216. The response to number 5 will indicate how well your child understands the season of Advent.

Match.

1. Magnificat

_____ Mary's cousin and the mother of John the Baptist

2. Angel Gabriel

_____ a time of preparation for Christmas

3. Advent

_____ Mary's prayer of praise

4. Elizabeth

_____ God's messenger to Mary

5. How will you care for others' needs this Advent?

_____

_____

_____

_____

FAMILY SCRIPTURE MOMENT

Gather and **Listen** to an Advent challenge, which Saint Paul wrote to the first Christians at Thessalonica.

May the Lord make you increase and abound in love for one another and for all, just as we have for you, so as to strengthen your hearts, to be blameless in holiness before our God and Father at the coming of our Lord Jesus with all his holy ones. . . . Finally, . . . as you received from us how you should conduct yourselves to please God–and as you are conducting yourselves–you do so even more.

1 Thessalonians 3:12—4:1

Share Invite family members to imagine that their guests this Christmas will be Jesus and several of their favorite saints. Ask: How might we prepare for their coming?

Consider for family enrichment:

■ Paul urges the Thessalonians not to "rest on their laurels" but to get ready for Jesus' second coming by increasing their acts of loving service.

■ By our Advent efforts to grow in holiness, we prepare a welcome for the Lord, who comes into our lives every day, as well as at the end of time.

Reflect and **Decide** What might it mean for us to "do even more" to please God? This Advent season, how will we show we are eagerly waiting for Jesus' coming?

Jesus, Mary, and Joseph, bless us and bless our families.

OUR LIFE

Jesus, Mary, and Joseph lived in Nazareth. The town was filled with small houses built close to one another. Most of the houses had flat roofs, where the people would sit and talk in the evening.

We can imagine what life must have been like for the Holy Family.

Every day Mary baked bread for her family. She served fruits and vegetables and sometimes fish or meat for dinner. Jesus, Mary, and Joseph prayed before and after each meal.

Joseph was a carpenter and taught Jesus how to use carpenter's tools. Mary and Joseph taught Jesus how to love, how to pray, and how to live according to God's law.

Just like families today, there were many times when Jesus, Mary, and Joseph laughed together. Sometimes they must have been sad. They must have talked about what the future might hold for Jesus.

Do you think Jesus, Mary, and Joseph did any of the things you do every day? Which ones?

SHARING LIFE

Imagine what it might be like if you could go back in time to visit the home of Jesus, Mary, and Joseph. Talk with your friends about what you would do. What might you say? Is there anything you would ask them to help you with?

93

Our Catholic Faith

We Celebrate Christmas

The Christmas season is a special time to remember and pray to the Holy Family. We celebrate the birth of Jesus, our Savior, in Bethlehem. We also celebrate other important feasts during the season of Christmas.

Holy Innocents

On December 28, we celebrate the feast of the Holy Innocents. The Holy Innocents were children whom King Herod ordered to be killed. Their story is told in the Gospel of Matthew.

When Jesus was born in Bethlehem, some visitors from the east came to King Herod in Jerusalem. They told Herod that a special star had guided them and that they had come to worship a baby born to be a king.

Herod was afraid of losing his throne to the newborn king. So he told the visitors to go to Bethlehem. He pretended that he wanted to know where the Child was, so that he could worship him, too.

The visitors found Jesus with Mary and Joseph. But they were warned by God in a dream not to tell King Herod. Joseph also had a dream. Joseph was told in the dream to take Mary and Jesus to Egypt for safety.

When King Herod realized that the visitors had tricked him and had gone home, he ordered his soldiers to go to Bethlehem and kill all boys who were two years old and younger.

Based on Matthew 2:1–16

Holy Family

On the Sunday following Christmas, we celebrate the feast of the Holy Family. We remember that Jesus, Mary, and Joseph lived together as a family in Nazareth.

There they worked, prayed, and played together. On the feast of the Holy Family, we ask Jesus, Mary, and Joseph to bless our families and to help us to live for the kingdom of God.

Mary, Mother of God

During the Christmas season, we celebrate a special feast to honor Mary as the Mother of God. On January 1, we remember that eight days after Jesus was born, Mary and Joseph took him to the Temple.

There the baby was named Jesus, the name the angel had given to Mary. The name Jesus means "God saves." We pray to Mary and remember that the Mother of God is our mother, too.

Epiphany

On the Sunday between January 2 and January 8, we celebrate the feast of the Epiphany. Epiphany is a word meaning "manifestation" or "showing forth." On this day we celebrate the showing forth of Jesus as the Light of the World. We hear the story of the wise men who came from a faraway land to worship Jesus, the newborn king.

COMING TO FAITH

Sometimes we think of Christmas as just December 25. But in the Church, the season of Christmas extends from Christmas Day to the feast of the Baptism of the Lord, the Sunday after Epiphany.

Form three groups. Each group will choose a way to share one of the feasts of the Christmas season. You can use music, drama, art, and of course, Scripture.

You might like to present your program to another group in your parish.

PRACTICING FAITH

A Christmas Prayer Service

Make a family Christmas ornament. Cut a decorative shape out of paper. Write on this shape the names of the people who make up your family. Then decorate your special ornament.

Opening Hymn

O come, all ye faithful, joyful and
triumphant,
O come ye, O come ye to Bethlehem;
Come and behold him, born the King
of angels;
O come, let us adore him,
O come, let us adore him,
O come, let us adore him,
Christ the Lord!

Leader: On the feast of the Holy
Family, we come together to honor
Jesus, Mary, and Joseph. We ask them
to bless our families with love, joy,
and peace.

Prayer Action

Each one reads the names on his or her
ornaments. Then each one places the
ornaments on a Christmas tree or
display stand.

Leader: Let us pray for our families.

All: Holy Family, help us to live as you
did. Help us to love and honor one
another in our families. Mary and
Joseph, help us to live together in
peace and love and to follow the way
of Jesus, our Savior. Amen.

Closing Hymn

O little town of Bethlehem,
How still we see thee lie!
Above thy deep and dreamless sleep
The silent stars go by;
Yet in thy dark streets shineth
The everlasting Light:
The hopes and fears of all the years
Are met in thee tonight.

Talk with your catechist about ways
you and your family can use the
"Faith Alive" pages together. You
might want especially to share the
meal blessing.

FAITH ALIVE AT HOME AND IN THE PARISH

In this lesson your fourth grader learned about some feasts in the liturgical season of Christmas. The Christmas season begins with the vigil Mass on Christmas Eve and ends with the feast of the Baptism of the Lord, the Sunday after Epiphany. During Christmas we celebrate the manifestations of Jesus Christ in our lives and in human history. Jesus is revealed to shepherds, to poor and simple people, and to strangers from the east. On the great feast of the Epiphany, we hear the story of the wise men's search for the newborn King of Israel. This story announces the epiphany, or manifestation, of God to all people. Finally, on the feast of the Baptism of the Lord, Jesus is revealed as God's own Son. Each of these feasts deepens our appreciation of God's great gift of Jesus.

Help your fourth grader to understand that Christmas is not just a one-day celebration, but an entire season. Encourage him or her to live in the spirit of the Christmas season by being a peacemaker at home, in school, and in his or her community.

A Family Christmas Banner

Design a banner that you can hang in your home during the Christmas season. Use a piece of felt about 3 feet x 4 feet. Hem the edges to make a casing for a dowel to hang the banner. The sample below might help you form ideas for your family's banner.

† A Meal Blessing

Let your blessing, dear God, come upon us. Bless this food also that it may become a holy meal we will share in love and fellowship.

May our sharing of this meal be like the sharing in Bethlehem where, through Jesus, we came to share your own life. Amen.

Learn by heart Faith Summary

- The Christmas season includes the feasts of the Holy Innocents, Holy Family, Mary, Mother of God, and Epiphany.

- The name Jesus means "God saves."

- The Holy Family is Jesus, Mary, and Joseph.

Go over the *Faith Summary* together and encourage your child to learn it by heart. Then help your fourth grader complete the *Review*. The answers to numbers 1–4 appear on page 216. The response to number 5 will show how well your child understands the Christmas season. When the *Review* is completed, go over it together.

Match.

1. The Holy Family

_____ His holy name means "God saves"

2. The Holy Innocents

_____ Jesus, Mary, Joseph

3. Herod

_____ children killed by Herod

4. Jesus

_____ the ruler of Jerusalem

5. Choose one feast of the Christmas season. What do we celebrate on this feast?

_____

_____

_____

_____

FAMILY SCRIPTURE MOMENT

Gather and ask: What are some things that might fill us with joy this Christmas? Then **Listen** to a letter of Saint John bearing God's joyful Christmas message to us.

What was from the beginning,…
concerns the Word of life—
… we have seen it and testify to it
and proclaim to you the eternal life
that was with the Father and was made visible to
    us—
… so that you too may have fellowship with us;
for our fellowship is with the Father
and with his Son, Jesus Christ.
We are writing this so that our joy may be
    complete.

1 John 1:1–4

Share Talk about the many ways that we can "see" and "touch" Jesus at Christmas. Who are the special people that can remind us of Jesus?

Consider for family enrichment:
◼ John's letter affirms that the Son of God became fully human, and that the first disciples are our witnesses to the incarnation.
◼ At Christmas we celebrate and become more alert to Jesus' presence in our lives.

Reflect and **Decide** Who might need to hear, see and touch Jesus this Christmastime? How will we help them to experience the presence of Jesus?

SUMMARY 1 ▪ REVIEW

Chapter 1—Living for God's Kingdom

- Jesus preached the good news of the kingdom of God.
- The kingdom of God is the saving power of God's life and love in the world.
- We build up the kingdom of God by working for love, justice, and peace in our world.

Chapter 2—The Virtues of Faith, Hope, and Love

- Faith enables us to believe and trust in God.
- Hope enables us to have full confidence in God, no matter what happens.
- Love enables us to love God, ourselves, and our neighbors.

Chapter 3—The Church, Jesus' Community

- The Church is guided by the Holy Spirit.
- The Church preaches, serves, worships, and lives as Jesus' community of faith, hope, and love.
- We become members of the Church through Baptism.

Chapter 4—The Beatitudes

- The Beatitudes teach us how to follow Jesus and be truly happy.
- The Holy Spirit helps us to live the Beatitudes.
- The Beatitudes are the spirit of love, mercy, and generosity required of Jesus' disciples.

Chapter 5—Living as Our Best Selves

- The Corporal Works of Mercy are ways we care for one another's physical needs.
- The Spiritual Works of Mercy are ways we care for one another's spiritual needs.
- As disciples of Jesus, we must live the Corporal and Spiritual Works of Mercy.

Chapter 8—Living as God's People

- God gave Moses the Ten Commandments to give to the people.

- The Ten Commandments help us to live with true freedom as God's people.

- The Ten Commandments help us to live the Law of Love, which Jesus taught.

Chapter 9—Living as Free People

- We can sin in thought, word, or action.

- Very serious sins are called mortal sins; less serious sins are called venial sins.

- A sin is mortal when what we do is very seriously wrong; we know that it is very wrong and that God forbids it; we freely choose to do it.

Chapter 10—God Is First in Our Lives

- The first commandment is "I, the LORD, am your God, who brought you out of . . . that place of slavery. You shall not have other gods besides me."

- Jesus taught us to put God first in our lives.

- When we live the first commandment, we live in true freedom.

Chapter 11—God's Name Is Holy

- The second commandment is "You shall not take the name of the LORD, your God, in vain."

- We live the second commandment by respecting God's name, the name of Jesus, and holy places.

- Cursing is wishing evil on someone. Swearing is calling on God to be our witness that we are telling the truth.

Chapter 12—We Worship God

- The third commandment is "Remember to keep holy the sabbath day."

- Christians celebrate their Sabbath on Sunday. We remember that Jesus rose from the dead on Easter Sunday.

- Catholics must take part in the Mass on Sunday or Saturday evening and on all holy days of obligation.

SUMMARY 1 ▪ TEST

Circle the correct ending.

1. Jesus preached the good news of
   a. the Romans.
   b. the kingdom of God.
   c. the apostles.

2. Faith, hope, and love are
   a. commandments.
   b. sacraments.
   c. virtues.

3. The Holy Spirit
   a. helped the Church only once.
   b. continues to help the Church today.
   c. never helped the Church.

4. The Works of Mercy are
   a. ways of caring for one another.
   b. ways of learning science.
   c. stories from the Old Testament.

5. The Beatitudes teach us
   a. about the rosary.
   b. to say our prayers.
   c. Jesus' way to be truly happy.

Complete the following sentences.

Sunday   Ten Commandments

Father   sin   first

6. God gave us the _____

_____ to help us live as God's people.

7. When we freely choose to disobey

God's law we _____.

8. When we follow the first commandment, we put God

_____ in our lives.

9. Jesus taught us to call God our

_____

10. Christians celebrate the Sabbath on

_____

Answer in your own words.

11. The kingdom of God means

_____

_____.

12. The Church lives as Jesus showed us when we _____

_____.

13. We follow the first commandment

when _____

_____.

14. We follow the second commandment when _____

_____

_____.

101

15. We follow the third commandment

when _____

_____

_____.

16. The virtue of faith is _____

_____.

17. The virtue of hope is _____

_____.

18. The virtue of love is _____

_____.

19. The Beatitudes help me to _____

_____

_____.

20. The Corporal and Spiritual Works of

Mercy help me to _____

_____

_____.

We are responsible for our choices.
List the steps you will take in
making good choices.

_____

_____

_____

_____

_____

_____

_____

Child's name _____

Your child has just completed Unit 2. Mark and
return the checklist to the catechist. It will help
both you and the catechist know how to help
your child's growth in faith.

_____ My child needs help with the part of the
Review/Summary I have underlined.

_____ My child understands the first three
commandments.

_____ I would like to speak with you. My phone
number is _____.

(Signature) _____

15 Loving Our Parents
The Fourth Commandment

Jesus, Mary, and Joseph, bless our family now and always. Amen.

Our Life

When Jesus was twelve years old, he went to Jerusalem with Mary and Joseph along with other family members and friends for the great Passover festival. After Passover, Mary and Joseph started home without Jesus. They thought he was returning with friends. When they discovered that he was not with them, Mary and Joseph rushed back to Jerusalem. After three days, they found Jesus in the Temple asking the teachers questions.

Mary was upset. She said, "Son, why have you done this to us? Your father and I have been looking for you with great anxiety."

Jesus said, "Why were you looking for me? Did you not know that I must be in my Father's house?"

Then Jesus went home with Mary and Joseph and was obedient to them.
Based on Luke 2:41–51

How do you think Mary and Joseph felt while they were looking for Jesus?

How do you show obedience to your parents or guardians?

Sharing Life

Work in two groups to develop your responses to these questions. Then share your ideas with everyone.

Group 1: Why should children obey the adults in their families?

Group 2: Why should we show respect to older people?

103

The Fourth Commandment

God did not make people to be alone. God created us to live as a family. In every family, some members care for those not yet ready or not able to care for themselves.

God wants us to honor and obey those who care for us and who are responsible for us. In the fourth commandment, God tells us, "Honor your father and your mother" (Exodus 20:12).

The Holy Family of Mary, Joseph, and Jesus worked and played, prayed and worshiped together. Mary, Jesus' mother, and Joseph, his foster father, taught him the Jewish prayers and God's commandments. They taught Jesus how to love and to care for others, especially the poor and people in need.

Jesus showed us how to follow the fourth commandment. For us, as for Jesus, to obey the fourth commandment means to love and honor our parents or guardians and all who care for us.

Our parents or guardians are our first and most important teachers. They teach us how to love God, others, and ourselves. When we honor and obey those who care for us, we are doing God's loving will for us. Doing God's will always makes us free and brings us true happiness.

Families are made up of people who belong to and care for one another. God wants all families to be happy, but some are not. Parents can have problems that lead them to live apart. When this happens, it might seem to their children that one or the other of their parents does not love them. This is not true.

If you feel this way, speak to your parents about it. You can also talk to a priest, your teachers, or another adult. Jesus does not want you to keep your hurts inside you.

To **honor** means to show respect and reverence for another.

Living the Fourth Commandment

We keep the fourth commandment by obeying all those who take care of us in any way. We respect our teachers and those who lead us. We respect our state and country by trying to be good citizens. A good citizen is someone who obeys the just laws of the country.

God wants us to honor our parents and those who care for us. We should help them in any way we can. When our parents get older, we must return to them the love and care they gave us as we were growing up. We must support and care for them. God wants all people to love one another as one family. When we do this, we are living for the kingdom of God as disciples of Jesus.

COMING TO FAITH

As friends, share together what obeying the fourth commandment means to you.

Tell what you would say to each person in these stories.

John's father has a very bad temper. Sometimes when he is angry, he hits John and his sister. John has just studied the fourth commandment. He wonders whether he can honor his father. He is confused about what to do.

Clara's grandmother has come to live with her family. She is old and does not like noise. Clara's mother has asked her not to play her stereo loudly. Clara is upset because she has to act in a special way now that her grandmother lives with her family.

PRACTICING FAITH

What do you think are important ingredients for a good family life?

Share your ideas with your group and make up a Family Life "recipe." For example, you might want to include ingredients like pounds of respect, cups of love, and tablespoons of honesty. What else needs to be mixed in?

LOVE

HONESTY

Family Life Recipe

_____

_____

_____

_____

_____

Talk with your catechist about ways you and your family might use the "Faith Alive" pages together. You might especially want to do a family blessing with family members. Then pray a favorite prayer with your catechist and friends.

In this lesson your fourth grader learned that the fourth commandment reminds him or her to love and honor parents, guardians, and all who care for us. However, the lesson was sensitive to situations that are far from ideal.

As a parent or guardian you have the responsibility to create a family atmosphere of shared love, honor, and respect that encourages your child to love and honor you. This can be a great challenge, especially when so many parents are working extra hard to keep their families going. Remember, too, to ask often for the guidance of God the Holy Spirit and the prayers of the Blessed Virgin Mary. Parents need to stress those virtues that are crucial to the Christian life: faith, hope, and love. By setting an example as you strive to live these virtues, you provide a natural way for your son or daughter to witness such virtuous living in action.

† A Family Blessing

Talk with your son or daughter about the ways he or she is important to you and your family. Then trace the sign of the cross on your child's forehead, while praying together:

† Jesus, Mary, and Joseph, be with us today. Help us to be a loving family. Help us to love and care for one another and all people. Bless our family now and always.

Learn by heart Faith Summary

- The fourth commandment is "Honor your father and your mother."

- Jesus showed us how to keep the fourth commandment.

- The fourth commandment teaches us to honor and obey all who take care of us.

Blessings from God

Write a prayer asking God for blessings that your family needs.

† Dear God,

Please give my family the blessings we most need:

_____

_____

_____

_____

Review
Go over the *Faith Summary* together and encourage your child to learn it by heart, especially the first statement. Then help your child complete the *Review.* The answers to numbers 1–4 appear on page 216. The last question will help you to see how well your fourth grader understands that being obedient brings us happiness and freedom. When the *Review* is completed, go over it together.

Complete the following sentences.

1. The fourth commandment is

"_____ your father and

your mother."

2. _____ and

_____ were the mother

and foster father of Jesus.

3. The fourth commandment teaches us

to respect our _____

and those who lead us.

4. The fourth commandment teaches us

to _____ older people.

5. How do you think obedience makes us free and happy?

_____

_____

_____

FAMILY SCRIPTURE MOMENT

Gather and ask: What do you think is the primary responsibility of parents? of children? Then **Listen** to a message for families.

Let the word of Christ dwell in you richly,…. And whatever you do,… do everything in the name of the Lord Jesus, giving thanks to God the Father through him. Children, obey your parents in everything, for this is pleasing to the Lord. Fathers, do not provoke your children, so that they may not become discouraged. Whatever you do, do from the heart, as for the Lord, and not for others….
Colossians 3:16–17, 20–21, 23

Share Invite your child or children to give one reason why it is hard to obey parents or guardians. Have each parent or guardian tell one way in which children can irritate them.

Consider for family enrichment:

■ In this letter to Christians at Colossae in Asia Minor, Paul urges family members to relate to one another in the spirit of Jesus with patience and love.

■ Good family relationships do not just happen. We have to work at them as essential to our Christian faith.

Reflect and **Decide** How will we as children try to be less irritating to our parents? How will we as parents try to make obedience easier for our children?

16 | Living for Life
The Fifth Commandment

Thank you, God, for the gift of all life!

Our Life

Look at the pictures. Write "Respecting Life" only in the boxes that show life being respected. Tell why you think this is so. Tell why life is *not* being respected in the other pictures.

What does it mean to respect life?

How do you show respect for all life, including your own?

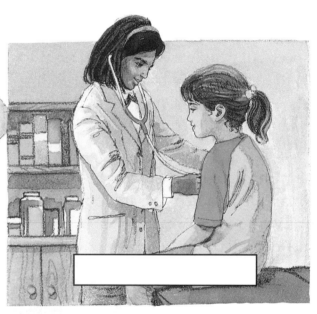

Sharing Life

Gather in a circle. Take turns responding to each question.

What things help us to be "for life"? What things work "against life"?

Tell some of the best ways to care for your own life.

Why do you think we should care about the lives of others?

The Fifth Commandment

From the Bible we know that God made all things good. Of all the living things that God made, people are the most special. That is because human beings are made in God's image and likeness. This means that people can think, choose, and love as God does.

Human beings are the only creatures on earth made in God's own image and likeness. Only human beings have God's own life in them.

God's word in the Bible teaches us that every person must be treated with respect. All people have an equal right to life, to freedom, and to be treated with justice. This is why God gave us the fifth commandment, "You shall not kill" (Exodus 20:13).

The fifth commandment teaches us that human life is sacred. We are to respect our lives and the lives of others. We must not kill or hurt ourselves or others.

We must not hurt our own bodies by taking drugs or by using alcohol to excess. We must care for our bodies by getting the right amount of rest, food, and exercise.

Jesus showed us how to live the fifth commandment. Jesus treated everyone the way he wants us to treat them—with kindness and patience. Jesus helped the poor and those who were suffering in any way. If people were being kept out by others, Jesus brought them into his community. He fought against all prejudice and discrimination.

Jesus told his followers that he "came so that they might have life and have it more abundantly" (John 10:10). Jesus is our lifegiver. He shows us all how to choose life.

Sacred means belonging to God. Human life is sacred because it belongs to God.

Choosing Life

The Church teaches that to choose life we must do much more than avoid committing murder and violent crime. Because we believe that all human life is sacred, we care about all people, especially those who are helpless.

Our Catholic faith reminds us of our special responsibility to care about and protect unborn babies, who cannot protect themselves. We care about the poor, those with special needs, and the elderly. We must respect, care for, and protect all human life. When we care for the needs of all people, we are helping to build a community of peace and justice in our world.

We choose life and live the fifth commandment when we care about all people and the world around us. If love is in everyone's heart, there is no room for the hate that brings about war.

We can work for peace by not being angry or jealous toward others. By keeping the fifth commandment, we do God's will and work for the kingdom of God.

COMING TO FAITH

Knowing the fifth commandment, what would you say about these stories?

Kenny likes playing computer games that have a lot of guns and violence. He says it does not hurt anyone.

Lisa says she doesn't see anything wrong with trying drugs just once.

Mark's father told him, "Don't talk to the new neighbors. They are not like us. They belong to a different race."

A chemical company is dumping toxic materials in a river. It's less expensive than handling them according to the law.

PRACTICING FAITH

Work together to write a song about respect for life. Choose an important "life" topic. Pick a tune you know and write your own words to it. You might share the song with your parish.

Then pray together in a life chain. Join hands and silently pray.

† Loving God, life is a beautiful gift. Help us to respect life in ourselves and in others.

End with your group song.

Talk with your catechist about ways you and your family might use the "Faith Alive" pages together. Spend some time talking with your family about life issues that affect all of you. Pray the Family Prayer with your catechist and friends.

FAITH ALIVE AT HOME AND IN THE PARISH

In this lesson your fourth grader learned that obeying the fifth commandment means choosing life. Ask her or him to tell you what this means for our own lives now.

All of life is like a "seamless garment" made out of only one piece of cloth. This means that if we treat any living thing badly, we hurt all living things.

We must respect and work for everyone's right to life. When we do this, we are doing God's loving will and living for the kingdom of God as Jesus' disciples. Unfortunately, violence is so rampant in our society that it sometimes shifts our focus from life and peaceful living to a life filled with anxiety.

To help your family and yourself be more conscious of choosing life and helping others to choose life, have a family discussion about the ways we can end the violence around us. Talk about ways that promote a loving respect for life, especially the life of the unborn.

The bishops in the United States have written a pastoral letter that shows the world how to work for peace and to keep the fifth commandment. It is called *The Challenge of Peace: God's Promise and Our Response.*

† Family Prayer

God, you have blessed each member of our family with the gift of life. We thank you for this gift and ask you to help us to treat one another with love and respect always. We pray this through Christ Jesus, our Brother and our Lord, who shows us how to respect all life. Amen.

Message about Life

Write a slogan for the blimp that tells something important about human life.

Learn by heart Faith Summary

- The fifth commandment is "You shall not kill." It teaches us that all human life is sacred.

- All people have an equal right to life and to be treated with justice.

- We choose life when we care for all people and the world around us.

Review

Go over the *Faith Summary* together and encourage your child to learn it by heart, especially the first and second statements. Then help your child complete the *Review*. The answers to numbers 1–4 appear on page 216. The last question will show you how well your fourth grader is beginning to understand the necessity of choosing life and not to squabble or to relish watching violence on television. When the *Review* is completed, go over it together.

Circle the letter beside the correct answer.

1. The fifth commandment teaches us

   a. not to kill or hurt anyone.

   b. to treat all living things with care.

   c. both a and b

2. The fifth commandment teaches us

   a. that it is wrong to hurt ourselves.

   b. nothing about ourselves.

   c. it is not wrong to damage our bodies with drugs or alcohol.

3. All human life is sacred means that

   a. needy people deserve care.

   b. unborn babies deserve our protection.

   c. both a and b

4. We live the fifth commandment by

   a. ignoring others.

   b. arguing and fighting.

   c. treating all living things with care.

5. How will you live the fifth commandment this week?

_____

_____

FAMILY SCRIPTURE MOMENT

Gather and invite family members to act out or describe situations in which a person needs physical help but the "rescuer" offers only words. Then **Listen** to Saint James' call to action.

So speak and so act as people who will be judged by the law of freedom. What good is it, … if someone says he has faith but does not have works? Can that faith save him? If a brother or sister has nothing to wear and has no food for the day, and one of you says to them, "Go in peace, keep warm, and eat well," but you do not give them the necessities of the body, what good is it? So also faith of itself, if it does not have works, is dead.

James 2:12, 14–17

Share what each one heard Saint James saying. Ask: Why do we sometimes fail to back up our words of encouragement with helpful actions?

Consider for family enrichment:

▪ By his clear teaching, James warns that Christian faith demands the works of love, otherwise faith is dead.

▪ Christian faith demands deep compassion for all those in need and tries to see that everyone has at least the necessities of life.

Reflect How might our parish show the needy that our faith is alive and well?

Decide How will we as a family take part in such Christian actions?

114

17 Faithful in Love

The Sixth and Ninth Commandments

Jesus, your love for us is always faithful. Teach us your ways.

Our Life

Karen had been sick for a long time but now her cancer was in remission. She was thinner and she had lost all her hair in chemotherapy. Karen was nervous about going back to school. How would her classmates react to her?

This is what happened:

- Some said, "Where is your hair? You look funny."

- Some were happy Karen was getting better, but they were uncomfortable and kept away from her.

- Some said, "You are really brave, Karen, and we love you." They made Karen part of everything they did.

Which ones were real friends to Karen?

What does it mean to be a faithful friend?

How do you show that you are one?

Sharing Life

Discuss these questions together.

Suppose this group had a friend like Karen. How would we act?

Is it always easy to be a faithful friend?

Do you think that Jesus wants us to be faithful friends? Why?

Being Faithful in Marriage

The love that a man and a woman share in marriage is very special. God made mothers and fathers to be equal partners. Married people share their joys and sorrows, their good days and bad days. God asks each woman and man who marry to be loyal and faithful to each other.

The differences between being a man and a woman are gifts from God. These gifts, our sexuality, are an expression of God's great love for us. Sexuality is very sacred and should be used responsibly. In the commandments, God reminds men and women that sexual love should be kept for marriage.

The sixth commandment says, "You shall not commit adultery" (Exodus 20:14). *Adultery* means being unfaithful to one's wife or husband. The ninth commandment says, "You shall not covet your neighbor's wife [or husband]" (Exodus 20:17).

The sixth and ninth commandments remind a married couple that no matter how difficult it is, a husband and wife must be faithful to their marriage vows as long as they live. Jesus reminds us that "'God made them male and female. For this reason a man shall leave his father and mother [and be joined to his wife], and the two shall become one flesh.' Therefore what God has joined together, no human being must separate."

Based on Mark 10:6–9

The sixth and ninth commandments also help a husband and wife to create a loving, caring community for their family. The Catholic Church teaches that married couples are to form a community of life and love together.

Families are the heart of God's wonderful world. It is in the family that we are first loved. Through family life, children learn how to do God's will—to love God, themselves, and others. Family members work together to bring about the kingdom of God.

Besides being faithful to our family, God also asks us to be faithful to ourselves. We do this when we love ourselves because we are made in God's image. Loving ourselves means respecting our bodies by what we say and think and do.

To be **faithful** means to be loyal and true to someone.

We remember that every part of our body is good. We do not do anything to our body or to another person's body that is disrespectful in thought or word or action.

We do not read books or see movies that dishonor our bodies. We do not allow anyone to do anything to us that would dishonor our bodies. Our bodies are a wonderful gift from God, made for true and faithful love in marriage.

Learning to be loyal and faithful friends is a good way to learn about love. You want your friends to be loyal, and you want to be loyal to them. This is true friendship.

You keep the sixth and ninth commandments in many ways. You love someone when you share your time with that person. You listen to and talk with each other.

Friendship also means that you give up what you want for what the friend wants when it is good for your friend. You try to be patient with your friends when they get on your nerves. You remember that no one is perfect, that everyone has faults and shortcomings.

117

COMING TO FAITH

Think of ways we can keep the sixth and ninth commandments right now in our lives. Role-play the following situations together.

Your older sister has gotten into trouble at school. Your parents are upset and are arguing with each other before dinner. You. . . .

One of your friends has a magazine with pictures you know you should not be looking at. Your friend tells you not to be a baby. You. . . .

PRACTICING FAITH

You are not yet ready to promise to be faithful to someone in marriage for life. But you *are* ready to be faithful to promises, loyal to family and friends, and respectful of your own body and the bodies of other people.

Share your ideas by completing each statement.

- *Faithful* means. . . .

- I can be faithful to my family by. . . .

- I can be a faithful friend by. . . .

- I can be faithful to myself by. . . .

Make up a group prayer about being faithful. Pray it together.

Talk to your catechist about ways you and your family might use the "Faith Alive" pages together. You might want to discuss the problems and solutions activity with a family member.

FAITH ALIVE AT HOME AND IN THE PARISH

This lesson explained the sixth and ninth commandments to your fourth grader. It is never too early to lay a foundation for faithful adult love by teaching children how to be faithful to God, to oneself, to family, to friends, and to promises made. It is imperative to teach them that sexuality is a great and beautiful gift of God's love.

Encourage your fourth grader to discuss any difficulties he or she may be having with others who may want to dishonor their bodies.

Teach them to avoid reading certain magazines or watching some television shows that tempt one to dishonor oneself or others.

Problems and Solutions

The chart below gives two examples of things that make it difficult to do what the sixth and ninth commandments ask of young people. Discuss these examples with your fourth grader, and then encourage him or her to add other examples.

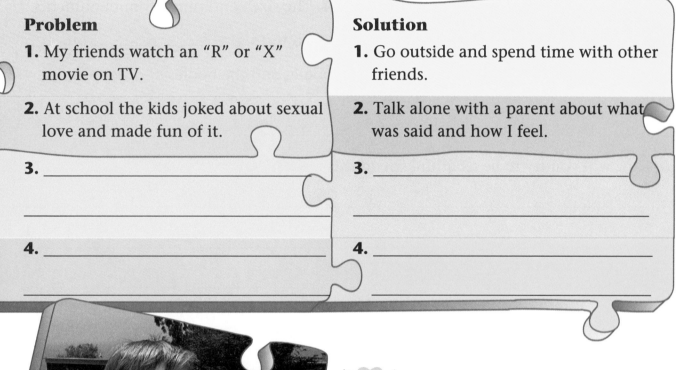

Problem

1. My friends watch an "R" or "X" movie on TV.

2. At school the kids joked about sexual love and made fun of it.

3. _____

_____

4. _____

_____

Solution

1. Go outside and spend time with other friends.

2. Talk alone with a parent about what was said and how I feel.

3. _____

_____

4. _____

_____

† Family Prayer

Jesus, you teach us how important it is to be faithful in love. Guide us in our daily lives to stay faithful to God, family, ourselves, and others.

Learn by heart

Faith Summary

- The sixth commandment is "You shall not commit adultery." The ninth commandment is "You shall not covet your neighbor's wife."

- We do not do anything to our own body or to another person's body that is disrespectful in thought or word or action.

- To be faithful means to be loyal and true to someone.

Review

Go over the *Faith Summary* together and encourage your child to learn it by heart, especially the first and second statements. Help your child complete the *Review*. The answers to numbers 1–4 appear on page 216. The response to number 5 will help you to see how well your fourth grader is beginning to develop the habit of faithfulness. When the *Review* is completed, go over it together.

Complete the following sentences.

1. Married people promise to love each other _____.

2. The ninth commandment is "You shall not covet your neighbor's _____."

3. The sixth commandment is "You shall not commit _____."

4. The sixth and ninth commandments teach us to _____ our bodies and the bodies of other people.

5. How will you try to be a faithful friend this week?

_____

_____

_____

FAMILY SCRIPTURE MOMENT

Gather and ask: What are some of the ways we show appreciation and respect for our bodies? Then **Listen** to a teaching from Saint Paul about our God-given bodies.

Avoid immorality. Every other sin a person commits is outside the body, but the immoral person sins against his own body. Do you not know that your body is a temple of the holy Spirit within you, whom you have from God, and that you are not your own? For you have been purchased at a price. Therefore glorify God in your body.

1 Corinthians 6:18–20

Share Invite family members to name something they like about their bodies. What does each one hear Saint Paul saying about our bodies as temples of the Holy Spirit?

Consider for family enrichment:

■ Paul wants the Corinthians to understand that sexual sins are an offense against God and against their own bodies.

■ We give God glory when we use our bodies in respectful and life-affirming ways.

Reflect What influences in our society are anti-Christian in their disrespect for the human body? How might we respond to them?

Decide What will we do to show that we respect our bodies and the bodies of other people as temples of the Holy Spirit?

18 Sharing Our Things
The Seventh and Tenth Commandments

Dear God, help us to share with people who are in need.

OUR LIFE

Luke was crazy about planes. He made models and sometimes went to air shows with his dad. He made a beautiful model for his school's science fair. He was very proud of it until a classmate brought in a remote control plane and showed how it could fly.

Luke had never been so envious in his life. How he wanted that plane! He knew it was far too expensive for his family to afford.

After the fair, Luke saw the plane and the remote control in the classroom. No one was near. He could take the plane. Who would know? Luke had never stolen anything before. But he wanted that plane so much!

Finish the story. What did Luke do? Have you ever wanted something that was not yours? What is the best way to fight such a temptation?

SHARING LIFE

Discuss these questions together.

Why is it wrong to steal?

What do you think God wants us to do when we are tempted to steal?

What do you think God wants us to do when others do not have the things they need to live?

121

Seventh and Tenth Commandments

God told the first created people to care for his gift of creation. We are responsible for everything in our environment. We are to share God's gifts in creation with others.

Since the sin of our first parents, people have been selfish and greedy and have not wanted to share. At times they even have wanted to steal their neighbors' possessions.

That is why God gave us the seventh and tenth commandments. The seventh commandment is "You shall not steal" (Exodus 20:15). The tenth commandment is "You shall not covet your neighbor's house . . . nor anything else that belongs to him" (Exodus 20:17).

Each time we steal, we break God's commandment. We have no right to take or damage or destroy what belongs to another, even if we know we will not be caught. We must also share our things with people less fortunate than we are.

The first Christians learned from Jesus how to do God's loving will for us. They would sell their possessions and distribute the money according to the needs of all. Today the Catholic Church challenges us to be faithful to Jesus' teachings. How wonderful it would be if all people had what they needed and were treated fairly and justly. When we help others to have what they need, we are helping to bring about God's kingdom of justice and peace.

The seventh and tenth commandments remind us not to do the following on purpose:

- steal things from others, or borrow things without permission;

- deliberately break or destroy other people's property without repairing or replacing it;

- cheat on tests or take the schoolwork of another;

- damage, write on, or paint on anyone's property;

- fail to take care of our possessions;

- be greedy and selfish about the things that are ours;

- be unfair or cheat others out of what is rightfully theirs.

Sometimes adults do things at their jobs that are against the seventh and tenth commandments:

- They steal things from the workplace or use the telephone all the time without permission to make personal calls. They are careless in their work or do not work for the time they are paid to work.

- Employers do not respect their workers when they pay them unjustly or do not give them clean and safe workplaces.

When all of us respect others and their belongings, we make the world a better place. We show we are living for God's kingdom.

FAITH WORD

Greed is wanting more than one's fair share or not wishing to share one's good fortune with others.

123

COMING TO FAITH

What would you say to each person in the following stories?

Jon and his friends like to spray paint pictures and words on walls and storefronts. "It's fun," he says, "and we never get caught."

"Everyone cheats," Dana says. "The teacher can't watch all of us. Besides, I'm getting good grades. Who gets hurt?"

Meg sees the pictures of the homeless families on TV. She tells you that she cannot do anything to help them. She says, "They live so far away. It's not my problem."

For the Needy

PRACTICING FAITH

Here is a very real and practical way to keep the seventh and tenth commandments. Decide what you can do together to help homeless children. Write your ideas below, then share them and come up with a group plan.

_____

_____

_____

_____

Talk with your catechist about ways you and your family might use the "Faith Alive" pages together. Maybe you could set up a family "Sharing Jar" as a way to care for others. Close by praying the Our Father with your catechist and friends.

FAITH ALIVE AT HOME AND IN THE PARISH

In this lesson your fourth grader has learned about the seventh and the tenth commandments. These commandments teach us to respect the possessions of others and the right of others to justice and equality. In addition, they remind us to care for the good things God has given us. These commandments reflect the profound social responsibility that our Christian faith gives us.

Sometimes it is difficult, particularly as adults, to avoid situations in which we might be tempted to steal. The virtue of justice demands that we respect the rights and property of others. Likewise, we are called to treat all living things with respect. In all our actions we strive to live as morally responsible children of God, ever mindful of our stewardship of the earth and its many gifts. Help your fourth grader to understand the meaning of the seventh and tenth commandments by doing the following activity with him or her.

Problem and Why It Is Wrong

Write why each of these problems violates the seventh or tenth commandment.

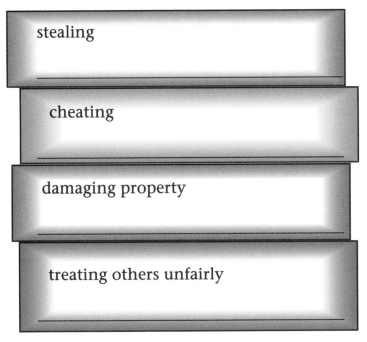

stealing

cheating

damaging property

treating others unfairly

Learn by heart ## Faith Summary

- The seventh commandment is "You shall not steal." The tenth commandment is "You shall not covet your neighbor's house . . . nor anything else that belongs to him."

- We are responsible for God's gift of creation.

- We must share with people less fortunate than ourselves.

A Family "Sharing Jar"

Help your fourth grader to think of others and their needs. Encourage all family members to contribute to a "Sharing Jar." When enough money has been put in the jar, involve the whole family, and especially your fourth grader, in buying a meal or some clothes for a needy family.

Go over the *Faith Summary* together and encourage your child to learn it by heart, especially the first statement. Then help your child complete the *Review.* The answers to numbers 1–4 appear on page 216. The response to number 5 will help you to see how your fourth grader is growing in unselfishness.

Circle the correct word or words.

1. The seventh commandment teaches us (to take only small things from others, not to steal).

2. The tenth commandment teaches us that it is wrong to (be greedy, enjoy the things we have).

3. Stealing is (borrowing with permission, taking without permission) things that belong to others.

4. Cheating is (stealing someone's answers, doing your own work) when you are taking a test.

5. We read in the Bible, "God loves a cheerful giver" (2 Corinthians 9:7). How will you be a cheerful giver this week to someone in need?

_____

_____

_____

 **FAMILY SCRIPTURE MOMENT**

Gather and **Listen** to Saint James' advice about true Christian wisdom.

Who among you is wise and understanding? Let him show his works by a good life in the humility that comes from wisdom. But if you have bitter jealousy and selfish ambition in your hearts, do not boast and be false to the truth. For where jealousy and selfish ambition exist, there is disorder and every foul practice. But the wisdom from above is first of all pure, then peaceable, gentle, compliant, full of mercy and good fruits, without inconstancy or insincerity.

James 3:13–14, 16–17

Share Have family members recall times when they were jealous of someone else's possession(s). (These recollections may be humorous or serious.) Ask: Would a wise Christian be jealous? Why or why not?

Consider for family enrichment:

■ James describes the truly wise person of any age as the one who does good deeds and acts unselfishly towards others.

■ We are wise in Christian faith when we share our possessions and avoid jealousy of every kind.

Reflect and **Decide** How will we as a family help one another to share what we have? to be truly wise?

19 Living and Telling the Truth
The Eighth Commandment

O God, make us true and sincere in all we say and do.

OUR LIFE

Once upon a time an emperor ordered a set of new clothes. The tailors did not want the emperor to punish them because the clothes they made were not beautiful enough. So they pretended to have special material that only "intelligent" people could see; ordinary people could not see it because it was really invisible. The emperor believed their story and asked them to make robes for him out of this wonderful material.

When the tailors said the robes were finished, the emperor "wore" them in a parade. The people, afraid to offend the emperor, shouted, "How beautiful the emperor's new robes are!" But a small child cried, "Mother, the emperor has no clothes!"

Why did everyone pretend to see the emperor's new robes?

Do you sometimes find it hard to tell the truth? Tell about it.

SHARING LIFE

Discuss these questions together. Why do people sometimes tell lies?

How can telling and living the truth help us to be free?

127

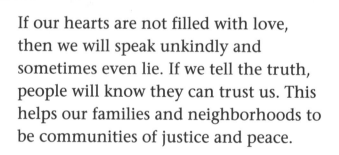

The Eighth Commandment

The eighth commandment that God gave Moses was "You shall not bear false witness against your neighbor" (Exodus 20:16).

To bear false witness means to lie. To lie means not to tell the truth. God wants us to speak the truth about ourselves and others. God also wants us to live the truth at all times. We live the truth by always doing God's loving and life-giving will for us.

Jesus always lived the truth in what he said and did. He told us, "If you remain in my word, you will truly be my disciples, and you will know the truth, and the truth will set you free" (John 8:31–32). When we live as disciples of Jesus, full of love, we are God's truthful people. To live the truth as disciples of Jesus is the best kind of freedom.

If our hearts are not filled with love, then we will speak unkindly and sometimes even lie. If we tell the truth, people will know they can trust us. This helps our families and neighborhoods to be communities of justice and peace.

Sometimes we lie about things we have done. We may not want to take responsibility for our actions. We may be afraid of being punished. At other times we lie or exaggerate about something we have or can do. We want others to think we are important, or "big shots."

Sometimes we lie about other people. Maybe we are jealous of them or do not like them. We make up a story that makes them look bad. We harm people each time we spread a lie about them.

We can also hurt someone by telling things about which we should be silent. This happens when we gossip or tell private or secret things about someone, things that would hurt that person if others found out. The eighth commandment teaches us that it is wrong to use even the truth to hurt others. Anyone who destroys another person's reputation must repair the damage done.

On the other hand, people might ask us to keep a secret about something bad that they are doing. We should not promise to keep such secrets. We need to speak to a parent, a teacher, or a priest, because keeping such secrets can hurt people.

If someone is drinking or taking drugs, he or she needs help. Keeping this a secret can lead the one who is doing something so harmful into serious trouble. In such cases, it is far more loving to tell the truth to someone who can help.

We can always choose to be truthful, no matter how difficult it is. The Holy Spirit helps us to tell and live the truth.

The choice is ours. If we ask, God the Holy Spirit will always give us the courage we need to be truthful. The Holy Spirit will help us follow the way of Jesus, who said, "I am the way and the truth and the life" (John 14:6).

A person who has the courage to tell and live the truth is a true follower of Jesus Christ. Such a person will also have the courage to speak out and further God's kingdom of justice and peace.

COMING TO FAITH

Knowing the eighth commandment, tell what you would do or what you would say to the people in these stories.

Justin has problems reading. After school he goes to special classes to learn to read better. One day at recess, Ryan tells you he found out that Justin has to go to the "slow class." Ryan wants to tell everyone. When you say it would be wrong, he answers, "Well, it's the truth, isn't it?"

Samantha tells you that she meets friends in the park each day. They give her pills that make her feel relaxed and happy. She asks you not to tell anyone.

Chris is very jealous of José, who is better in sports. One day, the principal announces that a gym window has been broken. Chris tells everyone that he saw José do it. This is not true, but now the whole school thinks José broke the window. Chris tells you that he was only fooling.

PRACTICING FAITH

Once a person spread harmful gossip and lies about someone. He told Saint Francis de Sales what he had done. Francis told him to empty a big feather pillow out the window and then gather up every feather. The person said this was impossible to do. The saint told him that it was just as impossible to restore the good reputation of the person lied about.

What will you do to be a more truthful person?

What will you do when you want to gossip? When you hear gossip?

Talk with your catechist about ways you and your family might use the "Faith Alive" pages. You might find time to say the Family Prayer together. Pray that prayer now with your catechist and friends.

FAITH ALIVE AT HOME AND IN THE PARISH

In this lesson on the eighth commandment, your fourth grader learned that God calls us to be truthful with others, both in our words and in our actions. We are called to correct any falsehood we may have started so as to protect the reputation of another.

Telling the truth demonstrates our concern for others, our love for our neighbor. It enables us to know the true freedom of God's children who are guided by the Spirit of truth. Jesus himself tells us, "If you remain in my word, you will truly be my disciples, and you will know the truth, and the truth will set you free" (John 8:31–32).

Talk with your child about times when he or she has found it difficult to tell the truth. Share your own experiences in this matter. Use the following list to guide the discussion.

We must tell the truth, even when we are tempted to lie for one of the following reasons:

- to avoid being punished for an accident, a mistake, or something we did wrong
- to get someone into trouble
- to make ourselves look important
- to get more of something than we deserve

As a family, talk about times when it is difficult to keep the eighth commandment.

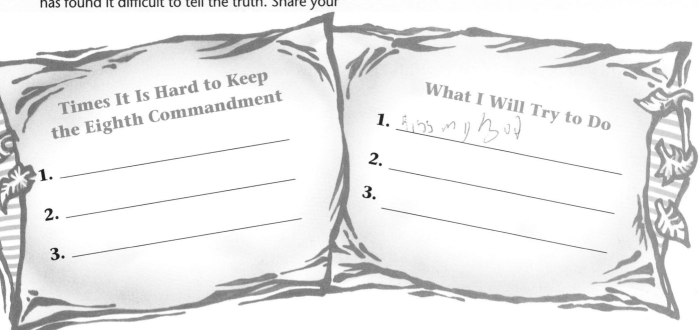

Times It Is Hard to Keep the Eighth Commandment

1. _____
2. _____
3. _____

What I Will Try to Do

1. _____
2. _____
3. _____

† Family Prayer

Say this prayer to ask the Holy Spirit to help you grow as a family in God's truth.

O God, help us to be:

A family that obeys God in everything
    and always does what is right,
whose words are true and sincere,
    and that does not spread lies
        about others.
A family that does no wrong to friends
    and does not spread rumors about
        neighbors.

Learn by heart Faith Summary

- The eighth commandment is "You shall not bear false witness against your neighbor."

- This commandment teaches us that it is wrong to lie, to tell someone's secrets, or to gossip.

- A person who has the courage to tell and live the truth is a true disciple of Jesus Christ.

Review

Go over the *Faith Summary* together and encourage your child to learn it by heart, especially the first statement. Then help your child complete the *Review.* The answers to numbers 1–4 appear on page 216. The response to number 5 will help you to see how well your fourth grader understands the importance of always being truthful. When the *Review* is completed, go over it together.

Circle the correct word or words.

1. The eighth commandment teaches us that we must not (spread gossip about, pray for) our neighbor.

2. We can tell lies (when it does not hurt anyone, never).

3. We try to develop the habit of being (truthful, lazy) so we will have the courage to speak up for and do what is right.

4. One should not promise to keep secrets if a person is (doing something harmful, a friend of ours).

5. How will you be one of God's truthful people this week?

_____

_____

_____

FAMILY SCRIPTURE MOMENT

Gather and ask: Have there been times when it was very hard to tell the truth? What did we do about it? Then **Listen** as Paul speaks of the "new you."

. . . put away the old self of your former way of life, corrupted through deceitful desires, and be renewed in the spirit of your minds, and put on the new self, created in God's way in righteousness and holiness of truth. Therefore, putting away falsehood, speak the truth, each one to his neighbor, for we are members one of another.

Ephesians 4:22–25

Share what it would mean for each of us to have new hearts and minds in Jesus.

Consider for family enrichment:

■ Paul reminds all Christians that in Baptism they have put on a new self in Christ. Living truthfully binds them together with others in the body of Christ.

■ By the grace of our Baptism, we have new hearts and minds. We have the power to speak and live the truth.

Reflect How can we help one another to be more truthful?

Decide Pray together: Jesus, You are the way, the truth, and the life. Be our strength when we are tempted to be untrue.

20 Preparing for Lent

O God, give me the strength to change what I should change.

OUR LIFE

Once there was a little caterpillar who thought she was the ugliest creature in the whole world. She was fuzzy and green. When she looked at her reflection in a puddle of water, she saw her six tiny eyes, six tiny legs, and all that fuzzy hair.

One day she curled up and went to sleep. As she slept, many changes took place.

After many weeks, the little caterpillar woke up. She found herself surrounded by a warm, soft cocoon. She pushed and pushed until the side of the cocoon broke open. Then she pulled herself out.

She looked in a puddle of water and saw the reflection of a beautiful butterfly. "Oh," thought the little caterpillar, "look how beautiful that butterfly is! It has two beautiful wings of blue and gold." The little caterpillar sighed and thought, "Oh, how I wish I looked like that." She was so sad.

As she raised her little caterpillar foot to wipe away her tears, she thought, "What's this?" A beautiful blue and gold wing had moved in front of her eyes. "It's me!" she realized. "I've turned into a beautiful butterfly!"

Then the butterfly, which had once been the ugliest caterpillar in the world, began to fly. She flew from flower to flower.

How do you think the butterfly felt?

SHARING LIFE

Discuss these questions together.

How can people change to make their lives more beautiful?

What changes can you make right now?

How does Jesus want us to change?

133

A Time for Change

The season of Lent is a time of change and growth. It is like springtime, when cocoons burst open and flowers begin to bud. It is a time for new beginnings. We try even harder to grow in our Catholic faith and to be better disciples of Jesus Christ. We prepare for the greatest celebration of the Church year, Easter.

During Lent we remember the promises of Baptism. We join in a special way with those who are preparing to be baptized at Easter and those who will receive the other sacraments of initiation, Confirmation and Eucharist.

Lent is a time for improving the way all of us live as God's people. We have to learn to be generous. Jesus told his disciples, "Whoever wishes to come after me must deny himself, take up his cross, and follow me."
Matthew 16:24

Jesus wanted the people to know that he was calling them to live as God's people. He told them: " The kingdom of God is at hand. Repent, and believe in the gospel."
Mark 1:15

Jesus brought us God's love and life. He offered up his life for the whole world and won for us the new life of his resurrection. Jesus brought us life that lasts forever.

A Time for Preparation

Each year during Lent, we prepare to celebrate Jesus' resurrection by remembering his life and death. We remember that it was through his death that Jesus entered into his resurrection and won new life for us.

As we prepare ourselves during the forty days of Lent, we remember that we have become part of Jesus' death and resurrection. By our Baptism, we have died to sin and have been given God's own life in Jesus Christ.

We prepare for Easter in many ways—by doing good works and by praying especially for those who will be baptized at Easter. We try to change the way we live our lives, even though we might fail from time to time. But always we continue to try and be better Catholics.

- We make sacrifices when we give things up. Lent is a good time for giving up things we do not need—for example, candy or watching TV.

- We do good works when we help other people. Many people give the money they save on candy and snacks to help the needy. Some people do this all year long.

- We take extra time for prayer during Lent. We pray the stations of the cross or the rosary every week.

COMING TO FAITH

Everyone has something hard or sad to face in life. Nothing is as difficult as the cross that Jesus had to bear. Still some things in life can be difficult for us. What is your difficult cross to bear? Perhaps it is an illness. Perhaps you have trouble at home or with friends. Maybe you have a problem that is keeping you from being your best self.

What do you think Jesus meant when he said that his followers should carry their cross and follow him?

Write how you can try to carry your cross this Lent.

_____

_____

Opening Song

Sing to the tune of "Kumbayah."

Lent is a time to change and grow.
Here we are Lord, help us know,
How to be your disciples true.
Oh, Jesus we follow you.

Opening Prayer

All: Jesus, this Lent, help us grow in our love of you and others. Help us to grow in the new life you have given us.

Reader: A reading from the book of the prophet Hosea (2:23–25).
"On that day I will respond, says the LORD;
  I will respond to the heavens,
  and they shall respond to the earth;
The earth shall respond to the grain,
  and wine, and oil, …
I will say … 'You are my people'."

The word of the Lord.

All: Thanks be to God.

Reader: A reading from the holy gospel according to John (12:24, 26).
Jesus says, "Unless a grain of wheat falls to the ground and dies, it remains just a grain of wheat; but if it dies, it produces much fruit. Whoever serves me must follow me…."

The gospel of the Lord.

All: Praise to you, Lord Jesus Christ.

Prayer Action

Leader: You will receive a seed and a cup filled with dirt. As you plant the seed, listen to these words. Think how you want to prepare yourself during Lent to share in Jesus' new life.

Jesus, you said that unless a seed dies, it does not produce other seeds. During Lent, Jesus, help me to "die" to:

- being selfish;
- saying things that hurt others;
- doing things that hurt others;
- being unfair to others.

Jesus, help your new life to grow in me so that I may:

- become more loving;
- care for others;
- say and do loving things;
- be a peacemaker.

Closing Hymn

Sing to the tune of "Kumbayah."

Jesus, help us to prepare
And please lead us to be aware
Of your new life that grows in us.
Loving Jesus, we do trust.

Talk with your catechist about ways you and your family might use the "Faith Alive" pages. You might especially enjoy creating a family changing tree.

FAITH ALIVE AT HOME AND IN THE PARISH

This week your fourth grader's understanding of Lent as a time to prepare for Easter was deepened. Lent is a time of spiritual renewal, of preparation for the sacraments of initiation by the catechumens of our parish. It is a time to reflect on the meaning of our lives and on the salvation that the suffering and death of Jesus gained for us.

The Lenten Scripture readings help us focus on our lives as disciples of Jesus Christ. We are challenged to review the patterns of our lives that are sinful and to renew our commitment to change our lives. We are called to reflect on the fact that through our Baptism we have become members of the body of Christ. We remember that by being baptized into the passion, death, and resurrection of Jesus, we have been made sharers in God's own life.

Help your fourth grader to decide on some change in his or her life in order to work for the peace and justice promised by God to all humanity. The following activity might help.

A Changing Tree

Find a large tree branch (or purchase a branch that is used for an Easter egg tree). Stand the branch in a large can filled with sand or dirt. Like the shape below, cut out colored blossoms, one for each family member. Ask your family to write one way they will try to change during Lent. Then fold each blossom to make a bud. Attach the shapes to the tree branch. On Easter open each bud to show how you and your family have bloomed during Lent.

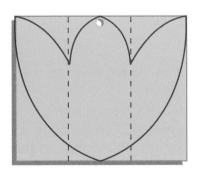

1. Divide paper in three equal sections.
2. Draw outline of blossom.
3. Cut out shape.
4. Write on the blossom.
5. Fold blossom and attach string through hole.

Learn by heart **Faith Summary**

- Lent is a time of preparation for Easter.

- We prepare for Easter by prayer, fasting, and good works.

† **Family Prayer**

As each one hangs his or her tulip bud on the tree, pray together:

Loving God, give us the courage to change and to follow Jesus more faithfully.

Go over the *Faith Summary* together and encourage your child to learn it by heart, especially the second statement. Then help your fourth grader complete the *Review*. The answers to numbers 1–4 appear on page 216. The response to number 5 will show how well your child is growing in understanding the meaning of Lent. When the *Review* is completed go over it together.

Circle T (true) or F (false)

1. Lent is a time after Easter. 　　　　　　　　　　　　　　(T)　　(F)

2. In Lent we are to think only of ourselves. 　　　　　　　T　　(F)

3. We prepare for Easter by prayer and good works. 　　　(T)　　F

4. Lent is a time of change and growth. 　　　　　　　　　T　　(F)

5. Tell one way you want to change during Lent.

_____

_____

_____

FAMILY SCRIPTURE MOMENT

Gather and ask: Who are the "stars" we admire? What values do they communicate? Then **Listen** to this Lenten call to "stardom" by Saint Paul.

Do everything without grumbling or questioning, that you may be blameless and innocent, children of God without blemish in the midst of a crooked and perverse generation, among whom you shine like lights in the world, as you hold on to the word of life, so that my boast for the day of Christ may be that I did not run in vain or labor in vain.

Philippians 2:14–16

Share Who might be today's stars in the eyes of Jesus? How do we hope to be more like them?

Consider for family enrichment:

■ Paul wants the Philippians to become "God's perfect children" by living blamelessly in the midst of a sinful society.

■ By our Lenten example of goodness, we can be a "message of life" for others in the name of Jesus.

Reflect What are some of the habits that keep us from shining like stars?

Decide as a family how we will help one another to overcome these habits during Lent.

21 | Celebrating Easter

Alleluia! Jesus is risen!

OUR LIFE

An Easter Play

Narrator: As our play begins, two people are walking together down a dusty road.

First Person: I never thought it would happen. Everyone loved Jesus so much.

Second Person: I know what you mean. I couldn't believe it when they told me that Jesus had been arrested.

First Person: Did you see him when they made him carry the cross?

Second Person: I kept thinking that something would happen, that someone would say, "Stop! Jesus should not be crucified!"

First Person: I heard him say, "Father, forgive them, they know not what they do," as they raised him on the cross.

Second Person: But now he is with us again. He has risen from the dead as he promised!

First Person: Many of my friends have already seen him. Some of them have sat at table with him and saw him break the bread.

Narrator: The friends of Jesus returned to their homes in Jerusalem. There they found the disciples of Jesus together. Everyone was saying:

All: Jesus is risen! Jesus is risen! Alleluia!

SHARING LIFE

What did you learn from Jesus' two friends?

Why is Easter so important to Christians?

Why should we be happy at Easter?

CHRIST IS RISEN

The Easter Triduum

All during Lent, we have been preparing to celebrate the most important time of the Church year, the Easter Triduum. Through our prayer, fasting, and good works, we are ready to remember the death and resurrection of our Lord and Savior, Jesus Christ.

Lent ends on Thursday of Holy Week. Then the Catholic Church gathers to celebrate the Triduum. The word *Triduum* means "three days." The Triduum begins on Holy Thursday with the Evening Mass of the Lord's Supper. It continues through Good Friday and Holy Saturday, and it ends with Evening Prayer on Easter Sunday.

At the Mass on Holy Thursday evening, we recall all that Jesus did at the Last Supper. We give thanks for the gift of the Eucharist and remember what Jesus taught us about serving others when he washed the feet of his apostles.

On Good Friday, we gather in the afternoon at a special liturgy to remember the passion and death of Jesus on the cross.

On Holy Saturday night, we begin and gather in darkness to celebrate the Easter Vigil. The word *vigil* means "keeping watch." We are watching for Christ our Light.

During the Easter Vigil liturgy, we bless the new fire and paschal candle, reminding us of the risen Christ. We hear God's word and then bless the baptismal water. We welcome new members into the Church community and celebrate new life through the sacraments of initiation and the renewal of baptismal promises.

The Easter Season

For fifty days after Easter we celebrate the resurrection of Jesus and our new life in him. This is the Easter season. It lasts from Easter to Pentecost Sunday.

Alleluia is the Christian song of Easter joy. It means "praise God" and expresses our great happiness at Jesus' victory over death and his risen presence with us.

Learn to sing the Easter Alleluia with your parish. Decorate the word here.

COMING TO FAITH

What is the most important time of the Church year?

_____

What do we remember at Easter?

_____

_____

The Easter candle is a symbol of the risen Christ, the Light of the World.

Practicing Faith

An Easter Prayer

Opening Hymn

Sing an Easter Alleluia.

Leader: Jesus Christ is the Light of the World. At Eastertime, let us thank Jesus for being with us always.

All: Jesus is risen, alleluia! All praise and glory to Christ our Light!

Leader: Bread that is grown from seeds in the ground becomes the Body of Christ. Grapes that are grown from seeds in the ground become the Blood of Christ.

Reader 1: Blessed are you, Lord, God of all creation. Through your goodness we have this bread to offer.

Reader 2: Blessed are you, Lord, God of all creation. Through your goodness we have this wine to offer.

All: Jesus, help us to recognize you when we take part in the Mass. During the Eucharistic prayer, help us to recognize you as your friends did after you rose from the dead.

Leader: Jesus Christ is the Light of the World. On this feast of Easter, let us thank Jesus for being with us always.

All: Jesus is risen, alleluia! All praise and glory to Christ our Light!

Closing Hymn

"Jesus Is Risen" (verse 2)

On this most holy day of days,
Let us together sing his praise!
Alleluia! Alleluia!
Raise joyful voices to the sky!
Sing out, ye heavens, in reply:

Alleluia! Alleluia! Alleluia!

Alleluia! Alleluia!

Talk with your catechist about ways you and your family might use the "Faith Alive" pages. If possible, share your Easter prayer with them.

FAITH ALIVE AT HOME AND IN THE PARISH

In this lesson, your fourth grader learned more about Easter. Saint Paul tells us, "If Christ has not been raised, your faith is vain" (1 Corinthians 15:17). Christians believe that the resurrection of Jesus is the culmination of God's liberation of humanity from sin and death. We have new life in the risen Christ.

This lesson provides the opportunity of deepening your child's awareness that the risen Christ is with us today in many ways, but especially in the Eucharist. Encourage your child to meet him there often and to recognize him as well in the poor, the hungry, and the homeless. Jesus himself said that whatever we do for the least of his sisters and brothers, we do for him (Based on Matthew 25:40).

† Family Prayer

Jesus, you are risen.

You are the Light of the World.

Fill us with your Easter joy.

Alleluia!

Learn by heart Faith Summary

- The Easter Triduum begins on Holy Thursday evening and ends on Easter Sunday evening.

- The Easter season includes the fifty days between Easter and Pentecost.

Living Our Faith

As Christians we are called to live our faith in the risen Christ by working for justice and peace. Plan with your family something you can do together, even in a small way, to show your faith. Write your ideas here.

_____

_____

_____

_____

Review

Go over the *Faith Summary* together and encourage your fourth grader to learn the summary by heart, especially the first statement. Then help your child complete the *Review*. The answers to numbers 1–4 appear on page 216. The response to number 5 will show how well your child understands the meaning of Easter. When the *Review* is completed, go over it together.

Answer.

1. What do we call the three special days before Easter?

_____

_____

2. What happened on Good Friday?

_____

_____

3. What do we celebrate on Holy Thursday?

_____

_____

4. What is our Easter song?

_____

_____

5. Why is Easter the greatest feast for Christians?

_____

_____

FAMILY SCRIPTURE MOMENT

Gather and list together signs of hope the family recognizes at this time of Easter. Then **Listen** as Peter shares his message of Easter hope.

Blessed be the God and Father of our Lord Jesus Christ, who in his great mercy gave us a new birth to a living hope through the resurrection of Jesus Christ from the dead, to an inheritance that is imperishable, undefiled, and unfading, kept in heaven for you. In this you rejoice, although now for a little while you may have to suffer through various trials.

1 Peter 1:3–4, 6

Share Ask: How does the risen Christ give us hope in our present crosses and trials?

Consider for family enrichment:

■ Peter's letter to the Gentile converts in Asia Minor reminds them that whatever abuse or misunderstanding they suffer for their faith will be rewarded by God.

■ Our hope is always in the risen Christ, no matter what trial or suffering comes our way.

Reflect and **Decide** What blessings do we hope God has in store for each of us? How will we try to be Easter blessings for people who are suffering in our faith community?

UNIT 3 ■ REVIEW

Loving Our Parents

In the fourth commandment God tells us, "Honor your father and your mother." The fourth commandment teaches us to honor and obey all those who care for us and to respect older people. We are to be good citizens and obey the just laws of our country.

Living for Life

God wants us to respect all living things. The fifth commandment is "You shall not kill." This commandment teaches us that human life is sacred. Human beings are made in the image and likeness of God. We respect and care for our bodies.

We live the fifth commandment when we care about life all over the world.

Faithful in Love

The sixth and ninth commandments help married couples to be faithful to each other. The sixth commandment is "You shall not commit adultery." *Adultery* means being unfaithful to one's wife or husband. The ninth commandment is "You shall not covet your neighbor's wife."

The sixth and ninth commandments teach us to respect our bodies and the bodies of other people. Loving others faithfully now prepares us to love someone forever in marriage.

Sharing Our Things

God wants us to share our good things with others. Because people can be selfish and greedy, God gives us the seventh commandment, "You shall not steal." It is wrong to take what does not belong to us. We must respect and treat with care things that belong to others.

The tenth commandment is "You shall not covet your neighbor's house . . . nor anything else that belongs to him." We must not be so jealous of another's things that we would steal or damage them if we could. If we want to follow Jesus, we work to see that all people have their fair share of what they need to live.

Living and Telling the Truth

God wants us to be truthful. The eighth commandment is "You shall not bear false witness against your neighbor." This commandment teaches us that it is wrong to lie, to tell someone's secrets, and to gossip.

UNIT 3 ■ TEST

Choose the correct ending.

1. The fourth commandment teaches us

   a. to obey those who care for us.
   b. to respect older people.
   c. to obey our parents.
   d. all of the above

2. When we love others faithfully, we

   a. love someone forever.
   b. obey the seventh commandment.
   c. obey the fourth commandment.
   d. all of the above

3. Stealing something that is not ours

   a. is wrong if we get caught.
   b. disobeys the seventh commandment.
   c. disobeys the fourth commandment.
   d. all of the above

4. The eighth commandment teaches us

   a. to honor our parents.
   b. to choose life.
   c. to be truthful.
   d. to be faithful in love.

Answer these questions.

5. How will you honor those who care for you?

_____

_____

6. How will you show respect for life?

_____

_____

7. How will you be a faithful friend?

_____

_____

8. Why is telling the truth important?

_____

_____

9. How will you care for others' things?

_____

_____

10. What is the fifth commandment?

_____

Child's name _Magally Gomez one_

Your child has just completed Unit 3. Mark and return the checklist to the catechist. It will help both you and the catechist know how to help your child's growth in faith.

_____ My child needs help with the part of the Review I have underlined.

_____ My child understands how the commandments help us to live as God's people.

_____ I would like to speak with you. My phone number is _____.

(Signature) _____

22 The Spirit Gives Us Life

Come, Holy Spirit, fill us with strength, courage, and peace.

OUR LIFE

Angela didn't want to see her Gram in the nursing home. She wanted things to be the way they used to be when Gram played games with her and drove her all over town.

She was afraid of seeing this Gram who now sat in a wheelchair and looked so feeble.

As Angela opened the door, she saw Gram sitting by the window. A tear trickled down her grandmother's cheek.

Angela was about to cry, too. Then she felt a surge of courage and a deep love for her Gram. She said in a clear voice, "Gram, I love you," and hugged her.

Where do you think Angela's new courage came from?

Who helps you to do difficult things? Explain.

There are many people in our lives who give us courage and strength in difficult times. Who are they?

What kind of power do these people give?

SHARING LIFE

Do you think that there is a power you cannot see or touch that helps people to do good? What is it?

Have you ever been given the power to make a hard decision? to do something brave? Tell about it.

Can you imagine times when God the Holy Spirit helps us to do difficult things?

The Gifts of the Holy Spirit

We know that the Ten Commandments, the Law of Love, the Beatitudes, and the Spiritual and Corporal Works of Mercy help us know the right things to do. But sometimes we are afraid to do the right thing, or we are confused about what is right and what is wrong.

That is why Jesus sends the Holy Spirit to each of us to be our Helper. Saint Paul tells us that God the Holy Spirit helps us make the right decision. Paul wrote that the one who has the Spirit is the person able to judge the value of everything.
Based on 1 Corinthians 2:15

God the Holy Spirit, the third Person of the Blessed Trinity, is with us today. The Holy Spirit first comes to us when we are baptized. By the power of the Holy Spirit, we are freed from sin and made members of the body of Christ. Now we can choose not to sin and to live as disciples of Jesus.

The Holy Spirit will also come to you in a special way in the sacrament of Confirmation. Confirmation unites us more strongly to the Father and to Christ and gives us a special grace to live the faith by our words and actions.

To help us, the Holy Spirit gives us special gifts. The Holy Spirit gives us these special gifts so that, like the disciples on the first Pentecost, we will have the courage we need to follow Jesus.

God the Holy Spirit helps us to make good choices. Filled with the Holy Spirit, we can try each day to do God's loving will in all that we say and do. To help us do this, we should pray this prayer to the Holy Spirit often:

† Come, Holy Spirit, fill the hearts of your faithful and enkindle in them the fire of your love. Send forth your Spirit and they shall be created and you shall renew the face of the earth.

Wisdom

Gives us the power to know what God wants us to do. It helps us to make the decision God wants us to make.

Understanding

Helps us to see how Jesus wants us to live in our world today. It shows us how we can help stop injustice and unfairness.

Right Judgment

Helps us to assist others in knowing what is right and how they can be courageous in doing it.

FAITH WORD

God's will is what God wants us to do. We can call it God's "loving will" because he always wants what is best for us.

Courage

Helps us to do God's loving will, even when we are afraid.

The Gifts of the Holy Spirit

Knowledge

Helps us to know our faith and what is needed to serve God.

Reverence

Helps us to show our love for God in all our thoughts, words, and actions.

Wonder and Awe

Helps us to put God first in our lives and to show respect for God's name, the holy name of Jesus, holy places and things.

Each of us needs the help of God the Holy Spirit to live as Jesus showed us. The Holy Spirit guides and directs the whole Church and each of us every day.

Coming To Faith

Name the gift of the Holy Spirit that you think each of the following people used most. Tell why.

Jean Donovan was a lay missionary who left her home to help the poor in El Salvador. Jean went because she felt she could help people there. She was murdered because of her work with the poor. We call her a martyr for her faith.

Armando's mom is one of the most respected people in the neighborhood. When people are upset and need to make a decision, they talk with her.

Name a special gift you have received from the Holy Spirit. How do you use this gift?

Name a gift of the Holy Spirit you might need today. Tell why.

Practicing Faith

Tell what you can do this week with the help of the Holy Spirit at home, at school, or in your parish or neighborhood.

Pray together the prayer to the Holy Spirit on page 151. Then sing.

Come, Holy Spirit, Creator blest,
And in our hearts take up your rest.
Come with your grace and heavenly aid
To fill the hearts which you have made;
To fill the hearts which you have made.

Talk with your catechist about ways you and your family might use the "Faith Alive" pages. Explain the gifts of the Holy Spirit to a family member. Say the Family Prayer to the Holy Spirit with your catechist and friends.

FAITH ALIVE AT HOME AND IN THE PARISH

Your fourth grader has learned in this lesson that Jesus did not leave us alone. He sent us the Holy Spirit to be our Helper, especially when we find it hard to do God's will. God the Holy Spirit is the third Person of the Blessed Trinity. As Catholics we believe that the Holy Spirit is guiding the Church and each person to do God's loving will and to grow in living for justice and peace.

Many Catholics have recently renewed their awareness of the central activity of the Holy Spirit in the Church and in their own lives. We can live the Christian life only by the power of God the Holy Spirit. The Holy Spirit moves us to pray, act, and live as Jesus calls us to do. The Spirit challenges us to be alert to situations that demand our attention as Christian people. Prompted by the Spirit, we remember that all of our prayers are directed to the Father, our Creator, through the Son, our Redeemer, and in the Holy Spirit, our Sanctifier.

You might ask yourself:

■ *How often do I show my family that the Holy Spirit is my Helper, especially when I am frightened or troubled?*

The Gifts of the Holy Spirit

Have your fourth grader write the names of the gifts of the Holy Spirit on slips of paper. Have each family member pick a gift and tell how he or she will ask God for it this week.

Help from the Spirit

Invite your fourth grader to explain the gifts of the Holy Spirit to you and your family. Use the following activity to help her or him to do this.

† Family Prayer

Come, Holy Spirit.
Help us to be wise.
Help us to be kind, patient, and brave.
Help us to bring your peace, your justice, your love, and your joy to those around us. Amen.

Learn by heart Faith Summary

- God the Holy Spirit fills each of us with special gifts.

- The gifts of the Holy Spirit are wisdom, understanding, right judgment, courage, knowledge, reverence, and wonder and awe.

- When we pray for guidance, God the Holy Spirit will help us to make the right choices.

Write how the Holy Spirit helps you. Use the large letters to begin each sentence.

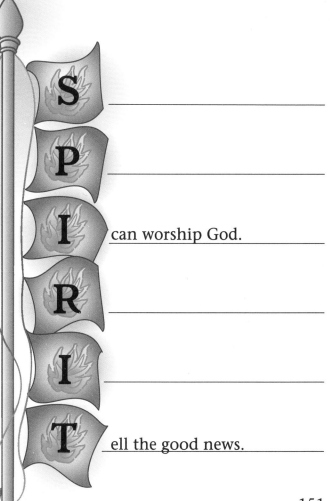

S _____

P _____

I can worship God.

R _____

I _____

T ell the good news.

Go over the *Faith Summary* together and encourage your child to learn it by heart, especially the second statement. Then help your child complete the *Review*. The answers to numbers 1–4 appear on page 216. The response to number 5 will help you to see how well your fourth grader understands the power that the Holy Spirit can be in his or her life. When the *Review* is completed, go over it together.

Circle the letter beside the correct answer.

1. The Holy Spirit gives help to

a. apostles only.

b. good, holy people only.

c. everyone.

2. The Holy Spirit helps us

a. by giving us everything we want.

b. by getting rid of all the hard things in our life.

c. every time we ask for help.

3. Which is *not* a gift of the Holy Spirit?

a. wisdom

b. courage

c. popularity

4. The gifts of the Holy Spirit

a. help us to get ahead in the world.

b. help us to live as followers of Jesus.

c. are just for adults.

5. What will you do this week to show that you are filled with the Holy Spirit?

_____

_____

FAMILY SCRIPTURE MOMENT

Gather and have family members name the gifts and talents they see in one another. Then **Listen** to Saint Paul describe the Holy Spirit as the source of all good gifts.

There are different kinds of spiritual gifts but the same Spirit; there are different forms of service but the same Lord. To each individual the manifestation of the Spirit is given for some benefit. . . . For in one Spirit we were all baptized into one body, whether Jews or Greeks, slaves or free persons, and we were all given to drink of one Spirit.

1 Corinthians 12:4–5, 7, 13

Share Ask: What gifts of the Spirit do we use for the good of all?

Consider for family enrichment:

■ Paul urges the Corinthians to recognize that, though there are different gifts, they are given for the good of all. Everyone in the Church has received the same Spirit.

■ The Spirit is present in each of us, enabling us to do our unique part in carrying on the mission and ministry of the Church in the world.

Reflect Do we recognize, appreciate, and affirm the spiritual gifts of others?

Decide How will we affirm and welcome the gifts of those in our parish who may be overlooked or taken for granted?

The Church Guides Us

O Holy Spirit,
thank you for
guiding the
Church in the
way of Jesus
Christ.

Our Life

Here are some pictures of our Church at work in the world.

Tell what you see the Church doing.

Name other ways the Church works for Christ's kingdom in the world.

Sharing Life

Discuss these questions:

Imagine yourself in any of these pictures. What would you be doing?

Imagine ways that your parish needs your help. How can fourth graders serve the Church?

Our Church Guides Us

Jesus called his disciples to be his Church and to carry on his mission in the world. The risen Christ sent the Holy Spirit to the disciples. The Holy Spirit helped them to become the body of Christ, the Church.

As members of the Church, we work together in our parishes and with all Catholics throughout the world. We help one another to continue Jesus' mission.

Today the Holy Spirit helps the Church continue Jesus' mission of preaching the good news and working for God's kingdom of justice and peace.

Each baptized person has something special to do to help carry on the mission of Jesus to the world. Saint Paul tells us, "There are different kinds of spiritual gifts but the same Spirit; there are different forms of service but the same Lord."
1 Corinthians 12:4–5

Some people are called to be leaders of our Church. First, there are our ordained ministers, our bishops, priests, and deacons. They serve by guiding the Church, helping us to worship God, and preaching the good news of Jesus.

The pope, the successor of Saint Peter, together with the bishops, leads the whole Catholic Church. The bishop is the leader of a diocese. A pastor is the priest who is the leader of a parish.

To share the work with our ordained ministers, the Spirit calls many other people to leadership positions in our Church. Your parish director of religious education and your catechists, for example, are called by the Holy Spirit to help the people of the parish know and live their faith. There may be other pastoral ministers in your parish, too.

In each parish, Catholics join together to hear and preach the good news of Jesus, to pray, to celebrate the sacraments, to serve others, and to help build up the kingdom, or reign, of God.

In order to help Catholics do these things together, we follow the laws of the Church. These laws are shown and explained in the chart on the next page. Study this chart carefully.

THE LAWS OF THE CHURCH

1.	Celebrate Christ's resurrection every Sunday and on the holy days of obligation by taking part in the celebration of Mass and by avoiding unnecessary work.	This means taking special time each week to think about God's goodness to us. We think about the ways in which we are to put God first in our lives.
2.	Receive Holy Communion frequently and take part in the celebration of the sacrament of Reconciliation. At a minimum, Catholics are also to receive Holy Communion at least once between the First Sunday of Lent and Trinity Sunday. We must confess at least once a year if we have committed any serious, or mortal, sins.	By celebrating these sacraments frequently, we grow in our love for God. The Holy Spirit guides us in making good decisions in our daily lives.
3.	Study Catholic teachings throughout our lives and continue to grow in faith.	Learning about our faith helps us to live it more each day. We will also be better able to carry on Jesus' mission.
4.	Observe the marriage laws of the Catholic Church. Make sure children receive religious instruction and formation.	Children need love and guidance from parents and others who care for them. They also need to learn about and live their faith in a loving family.
5.	Strengthen and support the Church, including our parish, priests, the whole Church, and the pope.	We have a responsibility to support the work of the Church and carry on the mission of Jesus Christ.
6.	Do penance, including fasting and not eating meat on certain days.	When we do penance, we give thanks for God's goodness.
7.	Join in the missionary work of the Church.	Each of us is called to help missionary work by giving what money we can and by praying for our missionaries.

Coming To Faith

Here are some things your parish church does to help you live for God's kingdom. Respond to each question.

- Your parish teaches you about God, Jesus, and the Holy Spirit through its religious education programs and the homilies at Mass.

Who helps you learn about your Catholic faith?

- Your parish invites members to volunteer for its various activities. The volunteers feed the hungry, take care of the lonely and the homeless, visit and pray with the sick, and reach out to people who are hurting.

How can you help care for others with your parish community?

- Your parish worships God and celebrates the seven sacraments.

How can you best take part in worshiping with your parish community?

How else does the Church help you live your Catholic faith?

Practicing Faith

Create an IDEAGRAM you would like to send to the pope, your bishop, or your pastor to tell him how the Church can help and guide you better. Also tell how you will help him to do this.

Share your ideagrams. Then develop a group letter that you will send to our Holy Father at the Vatican in Rome.

IDEAGRAM   (Circle one)

pope   bishop   pastor

Here are some ways I think you can help me to live my Catholic faith:

_____

_____

Here are some ways I will try to help you:

_____

_____

Talk with your catechist about ways you and your family might use the "Faith Alive" pages together. Ask family members to work with you on developing a family plan to help your parish. Pray the Family Prayer with your catechist and friends.

FAITH ALIVE AT HOME AND IN THE PARISH

Your fourth grader has learned in this lesson that he or she, though young, has a responsibility to carry on the mission of Jesus. Our Church, especially through our local parish, helps and guides us with the Beatitudes, the Ten Commandments, and the Spiritual and Corporal Works of Mercy that your child has already learned in previous lessons. One of the central teachings of the Second Vatican Council, echoing the earliest Christian communities, is that by Baptism all Christians are to participate in carrying on the mission of Jesus in the world.

In this lesson your child has also learned how the laws, or precepts, of the Church help us. These laws help us to live a moral and prayerful life as we seek to build up the kingdom of God. On the journey of faith, we are reminded by these laws of our minimum obligations in living the Catholic faith.

Making a Family Plan

Plan how your family can better help your parish continue Jesus' mission of preaching, worshiping, serving, and building up the community. Your plan might be something as simple as collecting food for the hungry or bringing up the gifts as a family at Mass.

Obeying the Laws

Ask your fourth grader to talk to you about the laws of the Church. Discuss one that he or she finds difficult to obey. Then do the activity together to help family members observe this law even more diligently.

This week I will try harder to keep this law of the Church:

This is what I will do:

Learn by heart Faith Summary

† Family Prayer

Holy Spirit, guide and direct all who belong to the Church. Help us to know and live the way of Jesus. Inspire our leaders to teach as Jesus taught. Build up our Church, Holy Spirit, so that all people will know, love, and follow the way of Jesus.

- The Holy Spirit guides the whole Church in continuing Jesus' mission.

- Each baptized person has something special to do to carry on Jesus' mission.

- The laws of the Church help us to live as good Catholics.

157

Review
Go over the *Faith Summary* together and encourage your child to learn it by heart, especially the first statement. Then help your child complete the *Review*. The answers to numbers 1–4 appear on page 216. The response to number 5 will help you to see how well your fourth grader is learning to serve others in your parish. When the *Review* is completed, go over it together.

Match the columns.

A   **B**

1. pastor   _____ successor of Saint Peter, together with the bishops, leads the whole Church

2. Holy Spirit   _____ ordained leader of the parish

3. pope   _____ rules that help us live as good Catholics

4. laws of the Church _____ helps and guides the Church

5. How will you try to serve others in your parish community?

_____

_____

_____

FAMILY SCRIPTURE MOMENT

Gather and ask: What prevents us from being more active as witnesses to our faith? Then **Listen** to Saint Paul's challenge to share our faith always.

. . . I remind you to stir into flame the gift of God that you have through the imposition of my hands. For God did not give us a spirit of cowardice but rather of power and love and self-control. So do not be ashamed of your testimony to our Lord, nor of me, a prisoner for his sake; but bear your share of hardship for the gospel with the strength that comes from God. He saved us and called us to a holy life, not according to our works but according to his own design and . . . grace.
2 Timothy 1:6–9

Share Imagine ways to share our faith with others outside the family and the parish.

Consider for family enrichment:

■ In this letter, Paul encourages Timothy, his young assistant, to overcome his fear and be brave in proclaiming the gospel.

■ By our Baptism and Confirmation, we have been empowered by the Holy Spirit to share our faith with all people.

Reflect and **Decide** How do we need to change in order to become powerful faith witnesses? Pray: Holy Spirit, move us and motivate us. Build Your holy fire in us! Help us to share our faith with all.

158

Jesus, help us to be strong when we are tempted to do wrong.

OUR LIFE

Joan dragged her feet all the way home. She was thinking about what her father was going to ask her and how she was going to answer. If Joan told the truth about the place she had been, she would be grounded for a week! It would be so easy to make up a story about. . . .

Finish Joan's story. What choice will she make? Will it be a good one?

Mr. Fisher was a tough teacher and no one wanted to have him in class. Some students called him names behind his back and made up stories about him. Kirk felt uneasy about this, but he wanted to be part of the group. Would he have any friends if he refused to listen to the gossip?

Finish Kirk's story. What will he do?

When you have to make a hard choice, how do you decide what to do?

SHARING LIFE

Share your story endings. Then discuss: Have you ever been in situations like those of Joan or Kirk? Who helped you to make choices?

How do you know whether you have made good decisions?

OUR CATHOLIC FAITH

Examining Our Conscience

Conscience is the ability we have to decide whether something is right or wrong. Our conscience is a gift from God. When our conscience is guided by the teachings of the Church, it helps us to know what is right and what is wrong.

Following our conscience means using what is in our mind and heart to make good decisions. Our thoughts and feelings are both important in helping us know what our conscience is telling us.

God the Holy Spirit speaks to us through our conscience. If we ask the Holy Spirit for help in making decisions, our prayers will be answered. To be good Christians we need to examine our conscience often.

We need to take time to think about ways we love God and others. We ask ourselves whether we have sinned by doing things that we know are wrong or by not doing the good things we should do. Each time we do this, we are examining our conscience.

We usually begin our examination of conscience by asking ourselves how well we have followed the Law of Love. We think of the ways we have been living for God's kingdom of justice and peace.

Then we think about how well we have tried to live the Beatitudes, the Spiritual and Corporal Works of Mercy, and the Laws of the Church. We ask ourselves whether we have obeyed the Ten Commandments. We have studied all of these this year and we can use them to help us.

When we examine our conscience, we may ask ourselves questions like those on page 161.

Before taking part in the sacrament of Reconciliation, or Penance, we examine our conscience so that we will know what sins to confess. The priest will then be able to give us advice about ways to live better.

In this sacrament we thank God for God's love and forgiveness. We tell God we are sorry for our sins. We ask God's help to do his loving will and to avoid those things that tempt or lead us to sin.

EXAMINATION OF CONSCIENCE

How have I shown love for God?

- Does God come first in my life, or are other things more important to me?

- Have I used God's name with respect, or have I sometimes said his name in anger?

- Have I remembered to pray regularly?

- Do I go to Mass on Sundays or Saturday evenings and on holy days of obligation and take part in the celebration? Or have I missed Mass for no good reason?

How have I shown love for others?

- Have I cared as Jesus wants me to care for the poor, the hungry, and those who are mistreated or oppressed?

- Have I done my best to try to live for the kingdom of God?

- Have I obeyed and been respectful to the adults who are responsible for me?

- Do I share my things with others, or have I been selfish? Have I taken others' things without permission?

- Have I been truthful and fair, or have I lied and cheated?

How have I shown love for myself?

- Have I taken care of my body by eating properly, getting rest, and not doing anything that could harm me?

COMING TO FAITH

A great thinker once said, "The unexamined life is not worth living." What do you think he meant by that?

When do you examine your life, your conscience? When should you?

How does examining your conscience help you prepare for the sacrament of Reconciliation?

PRACTICING FAITH

Take a few minutes to examine your conscience now. Use page 161 as a guide. Then gather together in a prayer circle.

Leader: Loving God, you call us to live as your people. Help us to follow your way of love.

All: Amen.

Reader 1: We will try to make good choices.

All: Help us to follow your way of love. (Make this response after each petition.)

Reader 2: We will be truthful. We will be honest. (**All:** Response)

Reader 3: We will be faithful. We will be obedient. (**All:** Response)

Reader 4: We will be fair. We will be peacemakers. (**All:** Response)

Leader: Let us pray the prayer Jesus taught us. Our Father. . . .

Talk with your catechist about ways you and your family might use the "Faith Alive" pages together. Pray the Family Prayer with your catechist and friends.

FAITH ALIVE AT HOME AND IN THE PARISH

In this lesson, your fourth grader has learned how, why, and when to examine his or her conscience. Have your child show you the questions used as an examination of conscience.

As an adult, it may be helpful for you to reflect on difficult choices you have had to make and the process you used when making these choices. Consider how and how often you examine your own conscience—not necessarily to highlight weaknesses but more to challenge yourself to greater vitality in living your Christian faith.

Stress with your child that a personal examination of conscience is done in quiet reflection. We do this in prayer with God, not apart from God. In our Catholic faith we have the custom of seeking the input and guidance of a spiritual director.

Examining Our Conscience

Encourage your child to think of how he or she has shown love for God, others, and self. Use the space below.

Examination of Conscience

How have I shown or failed to show:

Love for God?_____

_____

Love for others?_____

_____

Love for myself?_____

_____

Learn by heart Faith Summary

- Our conscience helps us to decide what is right or wrong.

- With the help of the Holy Spirit, we examine our conscience by asking ourselves how well we have lived God's law.

- We examine our conscience before celebrating the sacrament of Reconciliation.

† Family Prayer

God, the Holy Spirit, guide our family and give us the courage to make the right choices. Help us to remember the teachings of the Church and to say no to the choices that will hurt us or others. By choosing the right thing we will live God's law and live as disciples of Jesus.

163

Go over the *Faith Summary* together and encourage your child to learn it by heart, especially the first two statements. Then help your child complete the *Review.* The answers to numbers 1–4 appear on page 216. The response to number 5 will show you how well your fourth grader understands the need for examining his or her conscience. When the *Review* is completed, go over it together.

Use these words to complete the sentences.

practicing   Law of Love   Holy Spirit   conscience

1. Our _____ helps us to know what is right and wrong.

2. We examine our conscience by asking ourselves how well we have lived

God's _____, the Beatitudes, the Spiritual and Corporal Works of Mercy, and the Laws of the Church.

3. We form a good conscience by

learning and _____ what God wants us to do.

4. We pray to the _____ to help us form a good conscience.

5. Write one thing you will try to do better at home this week.

_____

_____

_____

FAMILY SCRIPTURE MOMENT

Gather and invite family members to share times when conscience has helped them to make a difficult decision. Then **Listen** to Saint Paul's advice about ways to let our inner treasure shine through.

. . .since we have this ministry through the mercy shown us, we are not discouraged. Rather, we have renounced shameful, hidden things; not acting deceitfully or falsifying the word of God, but by the open declaration of the truth we commend ourselves to everyone's conscience in the sight of God. For we do not preach ourselves but Jesus Christ as Lord, and ourselves as your slaves for the sake of Jesus. But we hold this treasure in earthen vessels, that the surpassing power may be of God and not from us.

2 Corinthians 4:1–2, 5, 7

Share Ask: What is your spiritual treasure? How do you want to share it?

Consider for family enrichment:

■ Paul urges believers to live honestly, avoid sin, and appreciate themselves as the human vessels who by God's power carry great spiritual treasure.

■ Jesus is the treasure that shines in us when we live by the word of God.

Reflect and **Decide** Who or what can strengthen our good conscience? What will we do to make our inner treasure more visible in the parish?

Dear God, help us to be forgiving and compassionate people.

Our Life

There once was a poor slave in Rome whose name was Androcles. He ran away from his cruel master and hid in a cave. Soon he fell asleep. A great noise suddenly woke him. A huge lion had come roaring into the cave. Androcles was terrified, but soon he noticed that the lion was limping badly. There was a large thorn in his paw. Androcles felt sorry for the lion. He picked up his paw. The lion leaned his head on Androcles' shoulder as if he knew Androcles would help him. Androcles pulled the thorn out quickly and the lion was so happy he jumped around like a puppy. That night the two slept side by side like two friends.

Eventually Androcles was captured. As a runaway slave, he was condemned to face the lions in the arena. He was led forth trembling, his eyes closed. The hungry lion rushed at him and to everyone's surprise, he lay down at Androcles' feet and rubbed his head against him. It was his old friend. The people were astonished. "Androcles and the lion must be set free!" they shouted. Many felt that the slave and the lion had taught them all how to live.

What is the lesson that Androcles and the lion taught?

Sharing Life

Talk together about things that can separate people from one another.

How can we be reconciled with one another? with God?

Forgiveness

All of us need to forgive and be forgiven. There are many times when we need to be reconciled, or united again, with people who hurt us. We need to forgive them. Jesus wants us to forgive others.

Jesus died to save us from our sins and to reconcile us with God and one another. Jesus wants us never to be separated from God by serious sin.

One time Peter asked, "Lord, if my brother sins against me, how often must I forgive him? As many as seven times?"

"Not seven times," answered Jesus, "but seventy-seven times" (Matthew 18:21–22). That was Jesus' way of saying that we must *always* forgive others.

God will help us to overcome sin in our world. By the sacrament of Baptism, we are set free from original sin. We share in God's own life, but we still need God's help to overcome our own sins

and sin in the world. But Jesus knew that sometimes we would sin. We would need God's forgiveness for the sins committed after Baptism.

Some sins are so serious that they separate us from God and from the Church. These are mortal sins. Reconciliation restores us to God's grace and reconciles us with the Church. While it is not absolutely necessary to confess venial sins, it is the good thing to do. It strengthens us and helps us to live closer to God.

Jesus gave his disciples the power to forgive sins in God's name. Jesus said to them, "Whose sins you forgive are forgiven them, and whose sins you retain are retained."
John 20:23

When we have sinned, God is always ready to forgive us. When we are sorry, we celebrate God's forgiveness in the sacrament of Reconciliation, or Penance.

The power to forgive sins in God's name has been passed on in our Church. In the sacrament of Reconciliation, our bishops and priests act in the name of God and of the Church to forgive our sins.

These are two ways we can take part in the celebration of the sacrament of Reconciliation: by ourselves with the priest (Individual Rite), or with others and the priest (Communal Rite).

During the celebration of Reconciliation, we may tell the priest our hurts and worries. The priest will give us good

Absolution is the prayer the priest says asking forgiveness of our sins.

The Individual Rite

- You make the sign of the cross with the priest. You may kneel behind a screen or sit and talk face-to-face with the priest.

- The priest or you may read a story from the Bible about God's love and forgiveness.

- You confess your sins to God by telling them to the priest. The priest talks to you to help you see how you can avoid sinning in the future.

- The priest gives you a penance. It may be a prayer to say or a good work to do for someone. Our penance helps us not to sin again.

- The priest asks you to pray an Act of Contrition to tell God that you are sorry and will try to sin no more.

- In the name of God and the whole Christian community, the priest absolves you from your sins. He extends his hand over your head as he prays the words of absolution.

- With the priest, you thank God for God's mercy and forgiveness.

advice and will try to help us. He will not tell anyone what we say, so we should not be afraid to talk to him about anything.

After celebrating this sacrament, we should promise God that we will try to avoid sin in the future. We should try also to be reconcilers and peacemakers in our daily lives by doing God's will and bringing God's peace to others. We can help others who may be fighting, hurt, or angry. We can be reconcilers in our home, in our school, and in our neighborhood. We can pray and work for justice and peace in our world.

COMING TO FAITH

When should people take part in the sacrament of Reconciliation? Why?

To take part in the sacrament of Reconciliation:

1. Examine your _____.

2. Tell your _____
to God through the priest.

3. Accept the _____
the priest gives you.

4. Be sorry and say an Act of

_____.

5. Receive _____
from the priest.

6. Remember to do your _____
and not to sin again.

PRACTICING FAITH

Plan with your group a parish flyer to be given out or a banner to be displayed in your church. Discuss the design and what the message will say to remind everyone of Reconciliation.

Talk with your catechist about ways you and your family might use the "Faith Alive" pages. Ask a family member to help you learn the Act of Contrition by heart. Then pray the Act of Contrition with your catechist and friends.

FAITH ALIVE AT HOME AND IN THE PARISH

Your fourth grader has reviewed how to celebrate the Individual Rite of the sacrament of Reconciliation. Talk to him or her about what happens in the sacrament. Share your own appreciation for the sacrament. Make sure he or she can pray an Act of Contrition from memory. Here are the words your son or daughter has learned.

Act of Contrition
My God,
I am sorry for my sins with all my heart.
In choosing to do wrong
and failing to do good,
I have sinned against you
whom I should love above all things.
I firmly intend, with your help,
to do penance,
to sin no more,
and to avoid whatever leads me to sin.
Our Savior Jesus Christ
suffered and died for us.
In his name, my God, have mercy.

Discuss with your family the steps below, which show how we celebrate the Communal Rite of Reconciliation.

THE COMMUNAL RITE

- We sing an opening hymn and the priest greets us. The priest prays an opening prayer.

- We listen to a reading from the Bible and a homily.

- We examine our conscience.

- We say an Act of Contrition together.

- We may pray a litany or sing a song, and then pray the Our Father.

- We confess our sins to a priest in private. In the name of God and the Christian community, the priest gives us a penance and absolution.

- We pray as we conclude our celebration. The priest blesses us, and we go in the peace and joy of Christ.

Learn by heart **Faith Summary**

- We celebrate God's mercy and forgiveness in the sacrament of Reconciliation.

- We can take part in the sacrament of Reconciliation alone with the priest or with the community and the priest.

- Jesus asks us to be reconcilers in our family, neighborhood, and world.

† **Family Prayer**
Decide when you will celebrate Reconciliation as a family. Pray the Act of Contrition together.

Review

Go over the *Faith Summary* together and encourage your child to learn it by heart, especially the first statement. Then help your child complete the *Review.* The answers to

numbers 1–4 appear on page 216. The response to number 5 will help you to see how well your fourth grader understands the way to celebrate the sacrament of Reconciliation. When the *Review* is completed, go over it together.

Use these words to complete these sentences.

God   forgiven   Reconciliation   alone   others

1. When we hurt someone, we want to

be _____.

2. We call the sacrament of Reconciliation a celebration because

we are happy that _____
always forgives us.

3. We can take part in this sacrament

_____ or with

_____ and the priest.

4. We celebrate God's forgiveness in the

sacrament of_____.

5. What will you do to celebrate the sacrament of Reconciliation more fully?

_____

_____

_____

FAMILY SCRIPTURE MOMENT

Gather and ask each family member to think about one personal victory over sin, evil, or wrongdoing. They may share if they wish. Then **Listen** to Saint John call Christians to victory.

Everyone who believes that Jesus is the Christ is begotten by God . . . . In this way we know that we love the children of God when we love God and obey his commandments. . . . And his commandments are not burdensome, for whoever is begotten by God conquers the world. And the victory that conquers the world is our faith. Who [indeed] is the victor over the world but the one who believes that Jesus is the Son of God?

1 John 5:1–5

Share What victory over sin or fear do I need at this time?

Consider for family enrichment:

■ Saint John urges Christians to overcome sin and division by choosing to obey the Law of Love. Their faith in Jesus gives them the power to be victorious over evil.

■ We show that we are God's children by our faith, hope, and love.

Reflect How might Reconciliation make us stronger "warriors" against sin and evil?

Decide When will we celebrate this empowering sacrament as a family?

26 ✝ We Celebrate the Eucharist

Jesus, help us
to recognize
you in all the
many ways you
are present in
our lives.

OUR LIFE

On the first Easter Sunday after Jesus had
risen from the dead, two of his disciples
were walking from Jerusalem to the
village of Emmaus. On the way they met
a man who began to walk with them. It
was Jesus, but they did not recognize
him.

The stranger began to explain the
Scriptures to the two disciples. He
showed how everything that had
happened to him had been spoken of
in the Old Testament. When they got
close to Emmaus, the men begged Jesus
to stay and eat with them.

When they sat down to eat, Jesus
broke the bread and gave it to them.
Immediately they recognized him in
the breaking of the bread. Then Jesus
disappeared from their sight.

The two disciples hurried back to
Jerusalem to tell the others that Jesus
had risen. They had come to know Jesus
in the breaking of the bread.
Based on Luke 24:13–35

How did the two disciples of Jesus
recognize him?

Do you feel close to Jesus when you
receive him in Holy Communion?

What do you usually say to him?

SHARING LIFE

Why do you think the two disciples did
not recognize Jesus at first?

Together with your group make a list of
times when we might not recognize
Jesus among us.

Discuss why we might miss him.

171

The Introductory Rites

As a worshiping assembly, we also recognize the risen Christ in the breaking of the bread. This is the Mass, and we begin the Mass with the sign of the cross. Our priest celebrant welcomes us and reminds us that the Holy Spirit is with us.

The priest then leads us in asking for God's mercy and forgiveness. We praise God by praying "Glory to God in the highest."

Liturgy of the Word

Now we listen carefully as God speaks to us through the different readings from the Bible.

The first reading is usually from the Old Testament. Then we sing or say a psalm. The psalms are songs of praise, thanksgiving, sorrow, and petition to God. Next we listen to letters, or epistles, written by Jesus' first disciples.

We stand to hear the gospel. The word *gospel* means "good news." In the gospel, Jesus speaks to us today, as he did to his friends long ago.

After reading the gospel, the priest or deacon explains the meaning of the Scriptures to us in a homily. Then we stand and pray the creed, a summary of our beliefs.

Next we say the Prayer of the Faithful. We pray for our Church and its leaders, for our needs and the needs of others.

The Liturgy of the Eucharist

Eucharist means "thanksgiving." We begin the Liturgy of the Eucharist by bringing gifts of bread and wine to the altar. These gifts stand for us and all we have.

The priest leads the entire assembly in the Eucharistic Prayer by asking the Holy Spirit to come upon our gifts to make them holy. The priest says and does what Jesus said and did at the Last Supper. The priest says over the bread, "This is my body." He says over the cup of wine, "This is the cup of my blood."

Through the power of the Holy Spirit and the words and actions of the priest, the bread and wine become the Body and Blood of Christ. This part of the Mass is called the consecration. After this, we proclaim the mystery of faith.

At the end of the Eucharistic Prayer, the priest prays,
"Through him,
with him,
in him,
in the unity of the Holy Spirit,
all glory and honor is yours,
almighty Father,
for ever and ever."
We answer, "Amen."

Next comes the Communion of the Mass. We pray together the Our Father as Jesus taught us. We share a sign of peace with one another to show we are trying to bring about the peace of God's kingdom.

This is followed by the breaking of the Bread, reminding us that we all share in the one Body of Christ. Now we can receive Jesus Christ, our Bread of Life, in Holy Communion. After Holy Communion, we think about the ways we can thank Jesus for giving us the gift of himself. We ask him to help us live as his disciples.

FAITH WORD

Liturgy means the official public worship of the Church.

Concluding Rite

As the Mass ends, the priest blesses us all in God's name. We make the sign of the cross and answer, "Amen."

The priest reminds us to live for God's kingdom of justice and peace. We hear him or the deacon say, "Go in peace to love and serve the Lord."

We answer, "Thanks be to God." We leave Mass prepared to continue living for the kingdom, or reign, of God.

COMING TO FAITH

What have you learned that will help you to take part in the Mass more fully?

Complete this prayer to be said after Holy Communion.

† Jesus, I believe you are with me. Thank you for loving me so much. Please help me live each day as your friend by. . . .

PRACTICING FAITH

Write a note to Jesus telling him how you will try to be his faithful disciple during vacation. Seal your note and hold it in your hand as you join your friends in a prayer circle.

Leader: Our time together is coming to an end. Let us give thanks to Jesus for all the gifts and graces we have been given this past year.

Person 1: Jesus, we bring a flower as a sign of our growing together with you.

Person 2: Jesus, we bring our *Coming to God's Love* book as a sign that we have grown as your disciples.

Person 3: Jesus, we bring you our notes as a sign of our love and our desire to stay close to you always.

Go around the circle. Each one in turn can express thanks for Jesus, for catechists, friends, parents, parish, and others. Begin by saying, "We thank you for. . . ."

Then sing together:

Now thank we all our God,
With hearts, and hands, and voices,
Who wondrous things has done,
In whom this world rejoices;
Who from our mother's arms
Has blessed us on our way
With countless gifts of love,
And still is ours today.

Conclude by sharing a sign of peace.

Talk with your catechist about ways you and your family might use the "Faith Alive" pages together. You might want especially to share your vacation plan with your family.

174

FAITH ALIVE AT HOME AND IN THE PARISH

This year your fourth grader has learned to come to God's love through the practice of the Law of Love, the Beatitudes, the Corporal and Spiritual Works of Mercy, the Ten Commandments, the Laws of the Church, as well as by prayer, celebration of the sacraments, and service to others. We have surveyed the whole horizon of Christian living—our Catholic morality and spirituality.

So that your child will continue to grow in faith, help him or her complete the "Vacation Time with God" below. Have your fourth grader check the things he or she will try to do, and encourage other ideas. Invite the other members of your family to make a plan, too.

I will love God by:

_____ praying each morning and night for God's help and forgiveness.

_____ taking part in the Mass with a joyful spirit each week.

_____ reading my favorite stories about God from this book, other books, or from the Bible.

Other ideas: _____

_____

I will love others by:

_____ forgiving those who hurt me.

_____ asking those who are ignored or made fun of to join me and my friends during our games.

_____ visiting or phoning an elderly, sick, or lonely person.

_____ helping my parish teach younger children about Jesus.

_____ not being mean or cranky.

Other ideas: _____

_____

I will love myself by:

_____ eating properly and getting enough sleep and exercise.

_____ not playing dangerous games.

_____ not joining children who do bad things or use drugs or alcohol.

Other ideas: _____

Learn by heart Faith Summary

- The Mass is made up of the Liturgy of the Word and the Liturgy of the Eucharist.

- We listen to readings from the Bible during the Liturgy of the Word.

- During the Liturgy of the Eucharist the bread and wine become the Body and Blood of Christ.

175

Go over the *Faith Summary* together and encourage your child to learn it by heart, especially the first statement. Then help your child complete the *Review.* The answers to numbers 1–4 appear on page 216. The response to number 5 will help you to see how well your fourth grader is growing in understanding that the Eucharist is to be lived out in our daily lives. When the *Review* is completed, go over it together.

Circle the letter beside the correct answer.

1. The Mass is our celebration of

   a. the sacrament of Reconciliation.

   b. Baptism.

   c. the Eucharist.

2. We listen to God's word from the Bible during the

   a. Introductory Rites.

   b. consecration.

   c. Liturgy of the Word.

3. We begin the Liturgy of the Eucharist

   a. by singing.

   b. by listening to Bible readings.

   c. with gifts of bread and wine.

4. At the consecration

   a. we listen to the gospel.

   b. the bread and wine become the Body and Blood of Christ.

   c. we say the Our Father.

5. After taking part in the celebration of the Eucharist, I will

_____

_____

FAMILY SCRIPTURE MOMENT

Gather and invite family members to name persons they love and are close to. Ask: How do we show that we are united with these loved ones? **Listen** as Saint John tells us how to be united with God.

He [Jesus] is expiation for our sins, and not for our sins only but for those of the whole world. The way we may be sure that we know him is to keep his commandments. Whoever says, "I know him," but does not keep his commandments is a liar, and the truth is not in him. But whoever keeps his word, the love of God is truly perfected in him. This is the way we may know that we are in union with him: whoever claims to abide in him ought to live [just] as he lived.

1 John 2:2–6

Share what each person heard from this reading.

Consider for family enrichment:

■ John assures the Christian community that Jesus forgives their sins and enables them to know God by obeying God's word.

■ In the Mass, Jesus makes us one with God and the worshiping community as we share the Word and the Eucharist.

Reflect and **Decide** How will we as a family try to grow in our faith during vacation time? Pray: Jesus, by your gift of the Eucharist, forgive us, guide us, make us one.

27 We Honor the Saints

All you saints of God, pray for us!

OUR LIFE

When the Nazi army invaded Poland in 1939, one of the first people they tried to silence was Father Maximilian Kolbe. Because of his courageous writing and preaching against the invaders, he was arrested and sent to Auschwitz, one of the worst of the Nazi concentration camps.

One July morning in 1941, the camp commander lined up all the prisoners. He told them that a man had escaped the night before. As a result, he selected ten people to be put in a dark bunker and left to die of starvation. One of the men began to plead with the commandant, "My wife, my poor children!" he cried.

Suddenly, Father Kolbe stepped forward. "Let me take the place of that man," he said.

During the terrible weeks that followed, those outside did not hear the usual screams and cries of despair. They heard the faint sounds of singing. When the bunker door opened on August 14, Father Kolbe was alive. He was still smiling when they killed him.

On August 14, 1982, Pope John Paul II named Maximilian Kolbe a saint of the Church.

Tell in your own words why you think Father Kolbe is a saint.

SHARING LIFE

Talk together about what the lives of the saints can teach us. How do you think they can help us?

Catholics believe that those who have died and who are in God's presence are still united with us. This is why we pray to the saints and ask them to help us.

Saints are women and men who have tried their best to do God's will and to be disciples of Jesus Christ. The saints are people like us who led holy lives.

The Church honors these men and women by canonizing, or naming, them saints. The Church tells us that they are with God in heaven.

A special day is sometimes set aside for remembering a saint each year. This day is called the saint's feast day.

By remembering the example of the saints, we learn ways to live our faith. By praying to them, we receive help to do God's will.

St. Cecilia

Patron Saints

Catholics often choose the names of saints for their children. We call these saints our patron saints. The Church also names saints to be patron saints of places or activities. For example, Saint Cecilia is the patron saint of musicians.

The patron saint of the United States is Mary, the mother of Jesus. We honor and pray to Mary under her title of the Immaculate Conception on December 8.

The patron saint of Mexico is Mary, Our Lady of Guadalupe (feast day, December 12). The people of Mexico remember and celebrate that Mary appeared to Juan Diego. Blessed Juan Diego was a poor Aztec Indian in Mexico. Mary asked him to have a church built in her honor at Guadalupe.

The patron saint of South America is Saint Rose of Lima (August 23). Her full name was Isabel de Santa Maria de Flores. She took the name Rose at Confirmation and lived in Lima, Peru, where she cared for the sick. Even while she was still living, many people asked for her prayers.

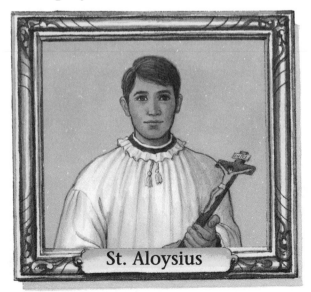

St. Aloysius

Does your parish have a patron saint? Write his or her name here:

_____

Some people pray to saints to ask them for help in their work. Saint Joseph, the foster father of Jesus, is honored on May 1 as the patron saint of workers.

Sometimes we pray to special saints for help in our studies. The patron saint of schools is Saint Thomas Aquinas (January 28).

Saint Aloysius Gonzaga is the patron saint of young people (June 21). Saint Aloysius was born in Italy. He taught religion to poor people and died at a very young age.

St. Frances Cabrini

Nurses pray to Saint Camillus (July 14). Saint Camillus ran a hospital in Rome. He became a priest and cared for the sick with special love.

Saint Frances Cabrini is the patron saint of people who leave home to go to a new land (November 13).

Saints were people just like us. They did the kinds of things that we do, too. There are women, men, and children who are living saints today. They follow the way of Jesus. They bring God's love to all people.

COMING TO FAITH

Explain why we honor the saints.

Can you be a saint? How?

Draw or paste a picture of your patron or favorite saint here. Write something about this saint.

A Prayer Service for Saints

Opening Song

Sing to the tune of "When the Saints Go Marching In."

Oh celebrate
With all God's saints.
They tried to do God's loving will.
They are the followers of Jesus,
Shining brightly in God's love.

Leader: We come together to celebrate the saints. Let us begin by praying to our patron saints.

All: (Each student names his or her patron saint. The other students say, Saint _____ , pray for us.)

Leader: Let us pray to the saints we have learned about this week. The response is "Pray for us."

Immaculate Mary, Mother of God, patron saint of the United States, ...

Our Lady of Guadalupe, patron saint of Mexico, ...

Saint Rose of Lima, patron saint of South America, ...

Saint Joseph, patron saint of workers, ...

Saint Thomas Aquinas, patron saint of schools, ...

Saint Aloysius Gonzaga, patron saint of young people, ...

Saint Camillus, patron saint of nurses, ...

Saint Frances Cabrini, patron saint of immigrants, ...

All you saints of God, ...

Leader: Let us honor the patron saint or special saint of our parish.

Reader: (One member of the group reads a report of the parish's patron or special saint.)

All: (Each person carries a picture or symbol of her or his patron saint to the front of the room and either places it on a table or hangs it on the bulletin board.)

Closing Hymn

Sing to the tune of "Holy, Holy, Holy."

Alle-Alle-luia
Celebrate the saints.
They follow Jesus and
Show us all God's love.
Alle-Alle-luia
All God's holy people
Help us to live our faith
And do God's loving will.

Talk with your catechist about ways you and your family might use the "Faith Alive" pages together. Say the Family Prayer with your catechist and friends.

FAITH ALIVE AT HOME AND IN THE PARISH

In this lesson your fourth grader was introduced to several saints of the Church. He or she learned that these people were canonized as saints because they modeled their lives on Jesus Christ. They tried to live as Jesus lived and to love as Jesus loved.

Fourth graders have a natural interest in these heroines and heroes of the Church. Remind your child that the saints were ordinary people like ourselves who simply tried to give their best to God. Help your child discover the unique gifts he or she has to offer God and others. The Second Vatican Council reminds us that every Christian by Baptism is called to holiness of life. All of us can be and should try to become saints.

Together with your child pray the words of the old hymn below that praises the saints who witnessed to Jesus before the world.

Learn by heart Faith Summary

- Saints are people who tried their best to do God's loving will.

- By remembering the saints and asking their help we learn to live our faith and to do God's will.

† Family Prayer

For all the saints who from their labors rest,
Who you by faith before the world confessed,
Your name, O Jesus, be forever blessed!
Alleluia, alleluia!

Following the "Stars"

The saints are like the stars of Christian faith. They light the way of living as Jesus' disciples. On the star below write one way the saints have taught you about being holy.

_____

_____

_____

_____

_____

Go over the *Faith Summary* and encourage your fourth grader to learn it by heart, especially the first statement. Then help your child complete the *Review*. The answers to numbers 1–4 appear on page 216. The response to number 5 will show how well your child understands the meaning of being a saint. When the *Review* is completed, go over it together.

Match the columns.

A	B
1. Saint Joseph	_____ the Church names a person a saint
2. Saint Rose of Lima	_____ a saint whose name someone shares
3. canonize	_____ patron saint of workers
4. patron saint	_____ patron saint of South America

5. Tell about a patron saint or a favorite saint.

_____

_____

_____

FAMILY SCRIPTURE MOMENT

Gather and ask: Who are the saints or holy people we wish we could invite to a family gathering? What might we have in common? Then **Listen** as Saint Paul describes God's family.

So then you are no longer strangers and sojourners, but you are fellow citizens with the holy ones and members of the household of God, built upon the foundation of the apostles and prophets, with Christ Jesus himself as the capstone. Through him the whole structure is held together and grows into a temple sacred in the Lord; in him you also are being built together into a dwelling place of God in the Spirit.

Ephesians 2:19–22

Share what special gift of holiness each one brings to this family.

Consider for family enrichment:

■ Paul assures the Gentile Christians that they are one family with the Jewish followers of Jesus. Together they are becoming God's dwelling place on earth.

■ We believe in the communion of saints—all the saints of every race, time, and place, both living and dead.

Reflect and **Decide** What is our family's next step toward holiness of life? How can we help our parish community to grow in holiness?

28 Mary and the Rosary

Mary, Queen
of the rosary,
pray for us.

OUR LIFE

One of the most beautiful and important gifts God has given us is memory. Imagine what it would be like to have no memory of our past. It does not matter whether our memories are happy or sad—we would be lost without them.

Take a minute now to name a happy memory you have. Then name a sad memory. If you can think of the most wonderful memory of all that you have, name that, too.

SHARING LIFE

Share some of your memories with your friends.

Sometimes we cannot remember people, but only stories about them. What do you remember about Jesus and Mary? Why are those memories important to you?

We Pray the Rosary

One of the prayers we say to the Blessed Virgin Mary is the rosary. The rosary helps us to remember the lives of Jesus and Mary. We begin the rosary by praying the Apostles' Creed on the cross of the rosary.

On the large bead and three smaller beads that follow, we pray one Our Father and three Hail Marys. This is followed by one Glory to the Father.

Then we pray the five decades, or five groups of ten beads. On the one large bead before each decade, we pray an Our Father. On each of the ten smaller beads, we pray a Hail Mary. At the end of each decade, we pray the Glory to the Father. The entire rosary concludes with the Hail, Holy Queen prayer.

Annunciation, by Dante Gabriel Rossetti, 1849

Mysteries of the Rosary

While we are praying the rosary, we think of events that took place in the lives of Jesus and Mary. We call these the mysteries of the rosary.

In the joyful mysteries, we think about the happy events in the lives of Jesus and Mary.

The Joyful Mysteries
- the annunciation
- the visitation
- the birth of Jesus
- the presentation of Jesus in the Temple
- the finding of Jesus in the Temple

We also remember the glorious times in the lives of Jesus and Mary.

The Glorious Mysteries
- the resurrection
- the ascension
- the descent of the Holy Spirit upon the disciples
- the assumption of Mary into heaven
- the coronation of Mary as queen of heaven

Sometimes we think of the sorrowful events in the lives of Jesus and Mary.

The Sorrowful Mysteries
- the agony in the garden
- the scourging at the pillar
- the crowning with thorns
- the carrying of the cross
- the crucifixion and death of Jesus

COMING TO FAITH

With a partner, take turns explaining how we pray the rosary.

What do the mysteries of the rosary help us to remember?

May is the month of our Blessed Mother. During this month Catholics honor Mary in many different ways. How can you show your love for Mary in a special way during May?

PRACTICING FAITH
A May Crowning

Opening Hymn

"Hail Mary"

Leader: Through the angel Gabriel, God asked Mary to be the mother of God's Son. "Mary said: 'Behold, I am the handmaid of the Lord. May it be done to me according to your word . . . .'" (Luke 1:38).

All: Holy Mary, pray for us.

Leader: Let us pray a litany to Mary. The response is "Pray for us."
Holy Mother of God, . . .
Mother of Christ, . . .
Mother of the Church, . . .

Leader: When Jesus was born in Bethlehem, shepherds came from the hills. They told Mary and Joseph about the angels who had appeared to them and had told them about this Child. "Mary kept all these things, reflecting on them in her heart."

Sinless Mother, . . .
Mother of Good Counsel, . . .
Mother of our Savior, . . .

Leader: When Jesus was dying on the cross, he saw his Mother and his friend John standing there. He said to John: "Behold, your mother."

Health of the sick, . . .
Comfort of the troubled, . . .
Help of Christians, . . .

Leader: Let us all gather around the statue of Mary. These flowers are a symbol of our love.

Crowning Ceremony

As everyone sings the closing hymn, one member of your group places a crown of flowers on the statue of Mary.

Closing Hymn

Immaculate Mary, your praises
   we sing.
You reign now in heaven with
   Jesus our King.
Ave, ave, ave Maria!
Ave, ave, ave Maria!

Talk with your catechist about ways you and your family might use the "Faith Alive" pages. You might pray a decade of the rosary together. Tell your family about the Mary Crowning you have shared with your friends.

FAITH ALIVE AT HOME AND IN THE PARISH

In this lesson your fourth grader was introduced to the rosary, an ancient Catholic devotion to Mary, the Mother of God. It is important that your child understand and appreciate this devotion as a part of our Catholic heritage. Your fourth grader has learned that the rosary is not simply a repetition of prayers but a meditation experience on the joyful, sorrowful, and glorious mysteries—special events in the lives of Jesus and Mary.

At Lourdes and especially at Fatima, Mary urged people to pray the rosary, especially for peace in the world. You might want to give your child a rosary if he or she does not already have one. Ask your parish priest to bless it.

† Family Prayer

Choose a mystery of the rosary. Share your thoughts about it. Then pray a decade of the rosary together thinking about that mystery.

Learn by heart Faith Summary

- The rosary is a special prayer Catholics pray to Mary.

- While we pray the rosary, we meditate on the joyful, sorrowful, and glorious mysteries.

Rosary for a Friend

Make a rosary for a friend in a hospital or nursing home. Use cord or yarn to string beads, buttons, or pasta. Use either a different color, size, or shape to indicate the Our Father and Hail Mary beads. Make a cross out of sticks or heavy paper to attach to the end of your rosary.

Go over the *Faith Summary* together and encourage your fourth grader to learn it by heart, especially the first statement. Then have him or her complete the *Review.* The answers to numbers 1–4 appear on page 216. The response to number 5 will show how well your child is growing in devotion to Mary. When the *Review* is completed, go over it together.

Write the word that goes with each description.

assumption   decade   rosary   visitation

1. A prayer to Mary in which we remember her joyful, sorrowful, or glorious mysteries.

_____

2. A joyful mystery in Mary's life.

_____

3. The group of ten small beads on each of which we pray a Hail Mary.

_____

4. A glorious mystery in Mary's life.

_____

5. Why do you think Catholics pray to Mary?

_____

_____

Gather and invite family members to describe who Mary is to them. Then **Listen** as a family to Saint Paul.

In the same way we also, when we were not of age, were enslaved to the elemental powers of the world. But when the fullness of time had come, God sent his Son, born of a woman, born under the law, to ransom those under the law, so that we might receive adoption. As proof that you are children, God sent the spirit of his Son into our hearts, crying out, "Abba, Father!"

Galatians 4:3–6

Share Ask: What difference might a real devotion to Mary make in our lives?

Consider for family enrichment:

■ Paul reminds Christians that through the incarnation of Jesus they have been made sons and daughters of God.

■ By saying yes to God's plan, Mary became the mother of Jesus and our mother, too.

Reflect What might we learn from Mary about living in true freedom as children of God?

Decide How will we grow as a family and as a parish in our devotion to Mary?

188

SUMMARY 2 ▪ REVIEW

Chapter 15—Loving Our Parents

- The fourth commandment is "Honor your father and your mother."

- Jesus showed us how to keep the fourth commandment.

- The fourth commandment teaches us to honor and obey all who take care of us.

Chapter 16—Living for Life

- The fifth commandment is "You shall not kill." It teaches us that all human life is sacred.

- All people have an equal right to life and to be treated with justice.

- We choose life when we care for all people and the world around us.

Chapter 17—Faithful in Love

- The sixth commandment is "You shall not commit adultery." The ninth commandment is "You shall not covet your neighbor's wife."

- We do not do anything to our own body or to another person's body that is disrespectful in thought, word, or action.

- To be faithful means to be loyal and true to someone.

Chapter 18—Sharing Our Things

- The seventh commandment is "You shall not steal." The tenth commandment is "You shall not covet your neighbor's house . . . nor anything else that belongs to him."

- We are responsible for God's gift of creation.

- We must share with people less fortunate than ourselves.

Chapter 19—Living and Telling the Truth

- The eighth commandment is "You shall not bear false witness against your neighbor."

- This commandment teaches us that it is wrong to lie, to tell someone's secrets, or to gossip.

- A person who has the courage to tell and live the truth is a true disciple of Jesus Christ.

Chapter 22 — The Spirit Gives Us Life

- God the Holy Spirit fills each of us with special gifts.

- The gifts of the Holy Spirit are wisdom, understanding, right judgment, courage, knowledge, reverence, and wonder and awe.

- When we pray for guidance, God the Holy Spirit will help us to make the right choices.

Chapter 23 — The Church Guides Us

- The Holy Spirit guides the whole Church in continuing Jesus' mission.

- Each baptized person has something special to do to carry on Jesus' mission.

- The laws of the Church help us to live as good Catholics.

Chapter 24 — Examining Our Conscience

- Our conscience helps us to decide what is right and wrong.

- With the help of the Holy Spirit, we examine our conscience by asking ourselves how well we have lived God's law.

- We examine our conscience before celebrating the sacrament of Reconciliation.

Chapter 25 — We Celebrate Reconciliation

- We celebrate God's mercy and forgiveness in the sacrament of Reconciliation.

- We can take part in the sacrament of Reconciliation alone with the priest or with the community and the priest.

- Jesus asks us to be reconcilers in our family, neighborhood, and world.

Chapter 26 — We Celebrate the Eucharist

- The Mass is made up of the Liturgy of the Word and the Liturgy of the Eucharist.

- We listen to readings from the Bible during the Liturgy of the Word.

- During the Liturgy of the Eucharist the bread and wine become the Body and Blood of Christ.

SUMMARY 2 ▪ TEST

Circle the correct ending.

1. The fourth commandment teaches us to

    a. go to Mass on Sundays.

    b. pray every day.

    c. honor those who care for us.

    d. respect human life.

2. The fifth commandment teaches us to

    a. respect all living things.

    b. obey our parents.

    c. tell the truth.

    d. be fair and just.

3. The sixth and ninth commandments teach us to

    a. go to Mass on holy days.

    b. say our prayers.

    c. study religion.

    d. be faithful in love.

4. The seventh and tenth commandments teach us to

    a. respect our bodies.

    b. tell the truth.

    c. respect others' belongings.

    d. confess our sins.

5. The eighth commandment teaches us to

    a. use the gifts of the Holy Spirit.

    b. tell the truth.

    c. obey the laws of our country.

    d. do our penance.

Complete these sentences.

consecrated   Reconciliation

pope   Bible   Holy Spirit

6. We celebrate God's forgiveness in the

sacrament of _____.

7. We listen to readings from the

_____ during the Liturgy

of the Word.

8. During the Liturgy of the Eucharist,

the bread and wine are _____.

9. God the _____ helps

and guides the whole Church.

10. The _____ is the

leader of the whole Catholic Church.

Write the number of the correct commandment.

11. _____ We speak up for the right to life of babies waiting to be born.

12. _____ A married couple is faithful to their marriage vows.

13. _____ We respect our parents, our teachers, and those who lead us.

14. _____ We care for things that belong to other people.

15. _____ We speak truthfully and kindly about others.

Answer these questions.

16. How do the Ten Commandments help us to live life as God wants?

_____

_____

_____

17. Name two gifts of the Holy Spirit.

_____

_____

_____

18. Write one law of the Church.

_____

_____

_____

19. How do Catholics celebrate God's forgiveness?

_____

_____

_____

20. Name the two main parts of the Mass.

_____

_____

_____

DAY OF RETREAT

Living the Ten Commandments

◀ OPENING ACTIVITY ▶

Choose teams to do this activity. Each team will be given a slip of paper on which is written a rule or a law. For example: "Keep off the grass." Team members will decide how to pantomime the rule, and then act it out for the whole group. Allow thirty seconds of "guessing time." Use a timer if you have one.

When all the pantomimes have been completed, look back over the rules or laws presented. Ask yourselves these questions:

- Is this rule (law) a good one or a bad one? Why?
- What kinds of rules or laws help us to live in true freedom?
- What kinds of rules or laws take away true freedom?

Share your thoughts as a group.

◀ **THINKING ABOUT GOD'S LAWS** ▶

Now talk about these questions with your team:

● How does keeping the commandments help you to love God? yourself? others?

Choose a team member to record on newsprint your team's responses. After five minutes, all the teams should come together to share responses. One person from each team should give a summary of what his or her team members said.

◀ PRAYER ▶

Leader: As disciples of Jesus Christ, we are all called to live the Ten Commandments. Living these laws will help us to become people of justice and peace and to love God, ourselves, and our neighbors as ourselves.

Reader 1: I am the LORD your God: you shall not have strange gods before me.

Reader 2: You shall not take the name of the LORD your God in vain.

Reader 3: Remember to keep holy the LORD's Day.

Reader 4: Honor your father and your mother.

Reader 5: You shall not kill.

Reader 6: You shall not commit adultery.

Reader 7: You shall not steal.

Reader 8: You shall not bear false witness against your neighbor.

Reader 9: You shall not covet your neighbor's wife [or husband].

Reader 10: You shall not covet your neighbor's goods.

All: God, be with us today as we think about the Ten Commandments and how they can help us to live as your disciples. We ask this in the name of Jesus Christ, who lives and reigns forever and ever. Amen.

◀ JOURNALING ▶

Take time now to think about God's laws in your own life. Let yourself become very quiet and still. Breathe deeply. Then think about the commandment that you find the most difficult to obey. Why do you think this is so? Would you like to do better with it? Do you think God will help you do better? What will you ask of God in prayer?

Write your thoughts as a prayer in your journal as quiet music plays in the background.

◀ PICTURE JOURNALING ▶

Divide into teams of five or six and choose one of the following projects:

● **Word Collage**

From poster board cut out a large circle. Decorate it to represent the earth. Then, on sheets of colored construction paper, write words that describe the feelings that come from following the Ten Commandments. Cut these words out and paste them to the "earth."

● **Footsteps to Follow Jesus**

On drawing paper sketch a path of ten footsteps. On each footstep write one of the commandments and how you or your group can live it.

● **Justice and Peace Collage**

On a large piece of poster board draw large block letters that spell out the word PEACE. Use magazines and newspapers to look for pictures that show people living the commandments. Cut out pictures that represent people doing acts of justice to bring about peace. Paste them within the word PEACE. Take time to have one person from each team explain the collages to the entire group.

◀ PRAYER SERVICE ▶

Leader: Loving God, living the Law of Love and following the Ten Commandments brings us true freedom. With this freedom we pray. . .

All: Loving God, fill us with your love and peace.

Leader: For the people in our world, that we can help one another to put God first in our lives, let us pray to the Lord.

All: Loving God, fill us with your love and peace.

Leader: For our Christian community, that we can help bring about God's kingdom of justice and peace, let us pray to the Lord.

All: Loving God, fill us with your love and peace.

Leader: For our parish family, that together we may grow stronger, wiser, happier, and more faithful in our lives as Catholics, let us pray to the Lord.

All: Loving God, fill us with your love and peace.

Leader: For our families, that we may show respect for other people who do God's will, let us pray to the Lord.

All: Loving God, fill us with your love and peace.

Leader: Loving God, when we obey out of love, we know the peace that comes from doing your will. Help us always to follow the road that leads to your peace. Amen.

Conclude by joining together as a group to sing a song of peace (for example, "Let There Be Peace on Earth").

SHARING OUR FAITH AS CATHOLICS

God is close to us at all times and in all places, calling us and helping us in coming to faith. When a person is baptized and welcomed into the faith community of the Church, everyone present stands with family and other members of the parish. We hear the words, "This is our faith. This is the faith of the Church. We are proud to profess it, in Christ Jesus our Lord." And we joyfully answer, "Amen"—"Yes, God, I believe."

The Catholic Church is our home in the Christian community. We are proud to be Catholics, living as disciples of Jesus Christ in our world. Each day we are called to share our faith with everyone we meet, helping to build up the kingdom, or reign, of God.

What is the faith we want to live and to share? Where does the gift of faith come from? How do we celebrate it and worship God? How do we live it? How do we pray to God? In these pages, you will find a special faith guide written just for you. It can help you as a fourth grader to grow in your Catholic faith and to share it with your family and with others, too.

Following the Church's teachings and what God has told us in the Bible, we can outline some of our most important beliefs and practices in four ways:

WHAT WE BELIEVE — CREED

HOW WE CELEBRATE — SACRAMENTS

HOW WE LIVE — MORALITY

HOW WE PRAY — PRAYER

CATHOLICS BELIEVE...

THERE IS ONE GOD IN THREE DIVINE PERSONS: Father, Son, and Holy Spirit. One God in three divine Persons is called the Blessed Trinity; it is the central teaching of the Christian religion.

GOD THE FATHER is the creator of all things.

GOD THE SON took on human flesh and became one of us. This is called the incarnation. Our Lord Jesus Christ, who is the Son of God born of the Virgin Mary, proclaimed the kingdom of God by his teaching, signs, and wonders. Jesus gave us the new commandment of love and taught us the way of the Beatitudes. We believe that by his sacrifice on the cross, he died to save us from the power of sin—original sin and our personal sins. He was buried and rose from the dead on the third day. Through his resurrection we share in the divine life, which we call grace. Jesus, the Christ, is our Messiah. He ascended into heaven and will come again to judge the living and the dead.

GOD THE HOLY SPIRIT is the third Person of the Blessed Trinity, adored together with the Father and Son. The action of the Holy Spirit in our lives enables us to respond to the call of Jesus to live as faithful disciples.

We believe in **ONE, HOLY, CATHOLIC, AND APOSTOLIC CHURCH** founded by Jesus on the "rock," which is Peter, and the other apostles.

As Catholics, **WE SHARE A COMMON FAITH.** We believe and respect what the Church teaches: everything that is contained in the word of God, both written and handed down to us.

We believe in the **COMMUNION OF SAINTS** and that we are to live forever with God.

I have also learned this year that to believe as a Catholic means

_____

_____

CATHOLICS CELEBRATE...

THE CHURCH, THE BODY OF CHRIST, continues the mission of Jesus Christ throughout human history. Through the sacraments and by the power of the Holy Spirit, the Church enters into the mystery of the death and resurrection of the Savior and the life of grace.

THE SEVEN SACRAMENTS are Baptism, Confirmation, Eucharist, Holy Orders, Matrimony, Reconciliation, and Anointing of the Sick. Through the sacraments, we share in God's grace so that we may live as disciples of Jesus.

By participating in the celebration of the sacraments, Catholics grow in holiness and in living as disciples of Jesus. Freed from sin by Baptism and strengthened by Confirmation, we are nourished by Christ himself in the Eucharist. We also share in God's mercy and love in the sacrament of Reconciliation.

CATHOLICS CELEBRATE THE EUCHARIST AT MASS. They do this together with a priest. The priest has received the sacrament of Holy Orders and acts in the person of Christ, our High Priest. The Mass is a meal and a sacrifice. It is a meal because in the Mass Jesus, the Bread of Life, gives us himself to be our food. Jesus is really present in the Eucharist. The Mass is a sacrifice, too, because we celebrate Jesus' death and resurrection and remember all that he did for us to save us from sin and to bring us new life. In this great sacrifice of praise, we offer ourselves with Jesus to God.

THE EUCHARIST IS THE SACRAMENT OF JESUS' BODY AND BLOOD. It is the high point of Catholic worship. It is a great privilege to take part weekly in the celebration of the Mass with our parish community.

I have also learned this year that to celebrate as a Catholic means

_____

CATHOLICS LIVE...

WE ARE MADE IN THE IMAGE AND LIKENESS OF GOD and are called to live as disciples of Jesus Christ. Jesus said to us, "Love one another as I have loved you."

When we live the way Jesus showed us and follow his teachings, we can be truly happy and live in real freedom.

To help us live as Jesus' disciples, we are guided by the Law of Love, the Beatitudes, and the Ten Commandments. The Works of Mercy and the Laws of the Church also show us how to grow in living as Jesus' disciples.

Together with our Jewish brothers and sisters and all Christians everywhere, Catholics try to obey and live by **THE TEN COMMANDMENTS**. These are the laws God gave to Moses to help God's people keep their covenant with God.

The first commandment tells us to keep God first in our lives.

The second commandment tells us to respect God's holy name and the holy name of Jesus.

The third commandment tells us to keep the Sabbath as a holy day. It reminds Catholics of our serious obligation to take part in Mass each week.

The fourth commandment tells us to love and honor our parents, guardians, and all who lead and care for us.

The fifth commandment tells us to respect all life, especially human life. We are to care for our bodies and treat others with kindness and respect.

The sixth and ninth commandments tell us to be faithful people. We are never to do anything to our bodies or the bodies of others that is disrespectful in thought, word, or action.

The seventh and tenth commandments tell us to be just and not to take what belongs to others. We are to share what we can with those less fortunate.

The eighth commandment tells us that we must be people who tell and live the truth and not lie or gossip.

As members of the Church, the body of Christ, we are guided by the **CHURCH'S TEACHINGS** that help us to form our conscience. These teachings have come down to us from the time of Jesus and the apostles and have been lived by God's people throughout history. We share them with millions of Catholics throughout the world.

Through **PRAYER AND THE SACRAMENTS**, especially Eucharist and Reconciliation, we are strengthened to live as Jesus asked us to live. In faith, hope, and love, we as Catholic Christians are called not just to follow rules. We are called to live a whole new way of life as disciples of Jesus.

In living as Jesus' disciples, **WE ARE CHALLENGED EACH DAY TO CHOOSE BETWEEN RIGHT AND WRONG.** Even when we are tempted to make wrong choices, the Holy Spirit is always present to help us make the right choices. Like Jesus, we are to live for God's kingdom, or reign. Doing all this means that we live a Christian moral life. As Christians we are always called to follow the way of Jesus.

I have also learned this year that to live as a Catholic means

_____

_____

_____

_____

CATHOLICS PRAY...

PRAYER IS TALKING AND LISTENING TO GOD. We pray prayers of thanksgiving and sorrow; we praise God, and we ask God for what we need as well as for the needs of others.

WE CAN PRAY IN MANY WAYS AND AT ANY TIME. We can pray using our own words, words from the Bible, or just by being quiet in God's presence. We can also pray with song or dance or movement.

WE ALSO PRAY THE PRAYERS OF OUR CATHOLIC FAMILY that have come down to us over many centuries. Some of these prayers are the Our Father, the Hail Mary, the Glory to the Father, the Apostles' Creed, the Angelus, the Hail Holy Queen, and Acts of Faith, Hope, Love, and Contrition. Catholics also pray the rosary while meditating on events in the lives of Jesus and Mary.

As members of the Catholic community, we participate in the great liturgical prayer of the Church, **THE MASS.** We also pray with the Church during **THE LITURGICAL SEASONS OF THE CHURCH YEAR**—Advent, Christmas, Lent, the Triduum, Easter, and Ordinary Time.

In prayer, we are joined with the whole communion of saints in praising and honoring God.

I have also learned this year that to pray as a Catholic means

_____

_____

_____

_____

By this time, you should know many of these prayers and practices by heart.

Our Father

Our Father, who art in heaven,
hallowed be thy name;
thy kingdom come;
thy will be done on earth
as it is in heaven.
Give us this day our daily bread;
and forgive us our trespasses
as we forgive those
who trespass against us;
and lead us not into temptation,
but deliver us from evil. Amen.

Hail Mary

Hail Mary, full of grace,
the Lord is with you;
blessed are you among women,
and blessed is the fruit
of your womb, Jesus.
Holy Mary, Mother of God,
pray for us sinners now
and at the hour of our death. Amen.

Act of Contrition

My God,
I am sorry for my sins with all my heart.
In choosing to do wrong
and failing to do good,
I have sinned against you
whom I should love above all things.
I firmly intend, with your help,
to do penance,
to sin no more,
and to avoid whatever leads me to sin.
Our Savior Jesus Christ
suffered and died for us.
In his name, my God, have mercy.

Glory to the Father

Glory to the Father, and to the Son,
and to the Holy Spirit.
As it was in the beginning,
is now, and will be for ever. Amen.

Apostles' Creed

I believe in God, the Father Almighty,
creator of heaven and earth.

I believe in Jesus Christ,
his only Son, our Lord.
He was conceived by the power
of the Holy Spirit
and born of the Virgin Mary.
He suffered under Pontius Pilate,
was crucified, died, and was buried.
He descended to the dead.
On the third day he rose again.
He ascended into heaven,
and is seated at the right hand
of the Father.
He will come again to judge
the living and the dead.

I believe in the Holy Spirit,
the holy catholic Church,
the communion of saints,
the forgiveness of sins,
the resurrection of the body,
and the life everlasting. Amen.

Morning Offering

O Jesus, I offer you all my prayers,
works, and sufferings of this day
for all the intentions of your most
Sacred Heart. Amen.

Grace Before Meals

Bless us, O Lord,
and these your gifts
which we are about to receive
from your bounty,
through Christ our Lord. Amen.

Grace After Meals

We give you thanks, almighty God,
for these benefits and all your gifts
which we have received,
through Christ our Lord. Amen.

Prayer to the Holy Spirit

Come, Holy Spirit,
fill the hearts of your faithful,
and enkindle in them
the fire of your love.
Send forth your Spirit and they
shall be created, and you shall
renew the face of the earth.

The Angelus

The angel of the Lord declared to Mary,
and she conceived by the Holy Spirit.
Hail Mary....

Behold the handmaid of the Lord,
be it done to me according to your word.
Hail Mary....

And the Word was made Flesh
and dwelled among us.
Hail Mary....

Pray for us, O Holy Mother of God,
that we may be made worthy of
the promises of Christ.

Let us pray:
Pour forth, we beseech you, O Lord, your
grace into our hearts that we to whom
the incarnation of Christ your Son was
made known by the message of an angel
may, by his passion and death, be
brought to the glory of his resurrection,
through Christ our Lord.
Amen.

Hail, Holy Queen

Hail, Holy Queen, Mother of Mercy,
our life, our sweetness and our hope!
To you do we cry, poor banished
children of Eve; to you do we send
up our sighs, mourning and weeping
in this valley of tears. Turn, then,
most gracious advocate, your eyes
of mercy toward us, and after this
our exile, show us the blessed fruit
of your womb, Jesus. O clement,
O loving, O sweet Virgin Mary!

Prayer for Vocations

Dear God,
You have a great and loving plan
for our world and for me.
I wish to share in that plan fully,
faithfully, and joyfully.
Help me to understand what it is
you wish me to do with my life.

- Will I be called to the priesthood
  or religious life?

- Will I be called to live a married life?

- Will I be called to live the single life?

Help me to be attentive to the signs
that you give me about preparing
for the future.

And once I have heard and understood
your call, give me the strength and the
grace to follow it with generosity and
love. Amen.

The Rosary

The Five Joyful Mysteries (by custom, used on Mondays, Thursdays, and the Sundays of Advent)

1. The annunciation
2. The visitation
3. The birth of Jesus
4. The presentation of Jesus in the Temple
5. The finding of Jesus in the Temple

The Five Sorrowful Mysteries (by custom, used on Tuesdays, Fridays, and the Sundays of Lent)

1. The agony in the garden
2. The scourging at the pillar
3. The crowning with thorns
4. The carrying of the cross
5. The crucifixion and death of Jesus

The Five Glorious Mysteries (by custom, used on Wednesdays, Saturdays, and the remaining Sundays of the year)

1. The resurrection
2. The ascension
3. The descent of the Holy Spirit upon the apostles
4. The assumption of Mary into heaven
5. The coronation of Mary as queen of heaven

Blessing and Giving of Ashes

Ash Wednesday is the first day of Lent. Catholics begin the Lenten season of penance by receiving blessed ashes. Ashes are an ancient sign of sorrow for sin and repentance. On Ash Wednesday the Church uses the ashes of palms left over from Palm Sunday of the year before. The ashes are blessed and placed on our foreheads in the shape of a cross with these or similar words:
"Turn away from sin and be faithful to the Gospel," or "Remember, you are dust and to dust you will return."

Blessing and Giving of Palms

The Sunday that begins Holy Week is called Passion, or Palm, Sunday. On Palm Sunday we remember the day on which Jesus rode into Jerusalem on a donkey and was greeted by the people with great joy. They welcomed Him as the Son of David, the Messiah. They broke off palm branches from the trees and waved them in the air. On this day, the Church blesses palms before Mass. The palms are given out to the people, who hold them during the reading of the gospel. Many Christians bring the palms home and keep them as a remembrance of the saving work of Jesus Christ.

The Stations of the Cross

There are fourteen "stations," or stops. At each one, we pause and think about what is happening at the station.

1. Jesus is condemned to die.
2. Jesus takes up his cross.
3. Jesus falls the first time.
4. Jesus meets his Mother.
5. Simon helps Jesus carry his cross.
6. Veronica wipes the face of Jesus.
7. Jesus falls the second time.
8. Jesus meets the women of Jerusalem.
9. Jesus falls the third time.
10. Jesus is stripped of his garments.
11. Jesus is nailed to the cross.
12. Jesus dies on the cross.
13. Jesus is taken down from the cross.
14. Jesus is laid in the tomb.

Blessed Sacrament

Catholics have a wonderful custom of going into the church to make a visit to Jesus in the Blessed Sacrament. The Blessed Sacrament is kept, or reserved, in the tabernacle for bringing Holy Communion to the sick and for worshiping Jesus Christ, who is truly present in the sacrament. We genuflect, or bend the right knee, toward the tabernacle before going into the pew. This is a sign of reverence for Jesus, who is present in the Blessed Sacrament. We can talk to Jesus about our needs, hurts, hopes, sorrows, and thanks.

Benediction of the Blessed Sacrament

Benediction is an ancient practice in the Church. The word *benediction* comes from the Latin word for "blessing." It is a gentle and peaceful ritual, reminding us that Jesus fills our lives with many blessings.

At Benediction a large Host, which was consecrated during Mass, is placed in a large holder called a "monstrance" so that all can see the Blessed Sacrament. The priest burns incense before the Blessed Sacrament. The incense is a sign of the adoration we offer in God's presence. The priest then lifts the monstrance and blesses the people. Each one makes the sign of the cross and bows in reverence before the Blessed Sacrament.

The Ten Commandments are found on page 59.

The Laws of the Church are found on page 155.

The Beatitudes are found on page 32.

The **Corporal and Spiritual Works of Mercy** are found on page 39.

An **Examination of Conscience** is found on page 161.

GLOSSARY

Absolution (page 167)
Absolution is the prayer the priest says asking forgiveness of our sins.

Apostles (page 200)
The apostles were the twelve special helpers chosen by Jesus to lead the first Christian community.

Baptism (page 27)
Baptism is the sacrament by which we are freed from the power of sin, become children of God, and are welcomed into the Church, the body of Christ.

Beatitudes (page 33)
The Beatitudes are ways of living that Jesus gave us so that we can be truly happy.

Blessed Sacrament (page 209)
Another name for the Eucharist. Jesus is really present in the Blessed Sacrament.

Catholic (page 27)
The Church welcomes all people and has a message for all people.

Confirmation (page 148)
Confirmation is the sacrament in which the Holy Spirit comes to us in a special way to give us courage to live as Jesus' disciples.

Conscience (page 160)
Conscience is the ability we have to decide whether a thought, word, or deed is right or wrong. We form our conscience according to the teachings of the Church.

Consecration (page 172)
The consecration is that part of the Mass in which the bread and wine become Jesus' own Body and Blood through the power of the Holy Spirit and the words and actions of the priest.

Corporal Works of Mercy (page 39)
The Corporal Works of Mercy are ways we care for one another's physical needs.

Covenant (page 71)
In the Bible, a covenant is a special agreement made between God and people.

Disciple (page 154)
A disciple is one who learns from and follows Jesus Christ.

Eucharist (page 50)
The Eucharist is the sacrament of Jesus' Body and Blood. Jesus is really present in the Eucharist. Our gifts of bread and wine become the Body and Blood of Christ at Mass.

Examination of Conscience (page 161)
An examination of conscience is asking ourselves, with the help of the Holy Spirit, how well we have obeyed God's law and have loved and served others.

Faith (page 20)
Faith is a virtue that enables us to believe and trust in God.

Faithful (page 117)
To be faithful means to be loyal and true to someone.

Free will (page 64)
Free will means that God gives us the freedom to choose between right and wrong.

Gifts of the Holy Spirit (page 148)
The seven gifts of the Holy Spirit are wisdom, understanding, right judgment, courage, knowledge, reverence, wonder and awe. They help us to live and witness to our Catholic faith.

God's will (page 149)
God's will is what God wants us to do. We can call it God's "loving will" because God always wants what is best for us.

Grace (page 200)
Grace is a sharing in the divine life, in God's very life and love.

Greed (page 123)
Greed is wanting more than one's fair share or not wishing to share one's good fortune with others.

Heaven (page 39)
Heaven is being with God and the friends of God forever.

Hope (page 20)
Hope is a virtue that enables us to have full confidence in God, no matter what happens.

Incarnation (page 200)
The incarnation is the mystery of God "becoming flesh," or becoming one of us in Jesus Christ.

Justice (page 122)
Justice means treating all people fairly.

Kingdom of God (Reign of God) (page 15)
The kingdom, or reign, of God is the saving power of God's life and love in the world.

Law of Love (page 21)
Love the Lord your God with all your heart, with all your soul, and with all your strength. Love your neighbor as you love yourself.

Laws of the Church (page 155)
The Laws of the Church are rules by which the Church helps us to live as good Catholics and disciples of Jesus.

Liturgy (page 173)
Liturgy is the official public worship of the Church.

Liturgy of the Eucharist (page 172)
The Liturgy of the Eucharist is one of the two major parts of the Mass. It is made up of the Presentation and Preparation of the Gifts, the Eucharistic Prayer, and Holy Communion.

Liturgy of the Word (page 172)
The Liturgy of the Word is one of the two major parts of the Mass. It is made up of readings from the Old and New Testaments, Responsorial Psalm, Gospel, Homily, Creed, and Prayer of the Faithful.

Love (page 21)
Love is the virtue that enables us to love God, ourselves, and our neighbors.

Mass (page 50)
Our celebration of the Eucharist, Jesus' special meal and sacrifice.

Original sin (page 166)
Original sin is the first sin of humankind. Every human being is born with and suffers from the effects of this sin.

Penance (page 167)
We receive a penance from the priest in the sacrament of Reconciliation. Our penance helps to make up for the hurt caused by our sins and helps us to avoid sin in the future. Our penance can be a prayer or good deed.

Pope (page 154)
The pope is the bishop of Rome. He is the successor of Saint Peter and the leader of the whole Catholic Church.

Prayer (page 204)
Prayer is directing one's heart and mind to God. In prayer we talk and listen to God.

Reconciliation (page 166)
Reconciliation is the sacrament in which we celebrate God's love and forgiveness of our sins.

Respect (page 77)
To respect means to show honor to someone or something.

Sabbath (page 83)
The word *Sabbath* comes from a Jewish word that means "rest." From the beginning of the Church, Christians have celebrated their Sabbath on Sunday.

Sacrament (page 155)
The sacraments are powerful signs through which Jesus Christ shares God's life and love with us in the community of the Church.

Sacred (page 111)
Sacred means belonging to God. Human life is sacred because it belongs to God.

Sin (page 65)
Sin is freely choosing to do what we know is wrong. When we sin, we disobey God's law on purpose.

Spiritual Works of Mercy (page 39)
The Spiritual Works of Mercy are ways we care for one another's spiritual needs.

Temptation (page 64)
A temptation is a strong feeling to do or to want something wrong. Temptations are not sins.

Ten Commandments (page 58)
The Ten Commandments are laws given to us by God to help us live as God's people. God gave the Ten Commandments to Moses on Mount Sinai.

Virtue (page 21)
A virtue is the habit of doing good.

Vocation (page 154)
A vocation is our call to live holy lives of service in our Church and in our world.

Witness (page 27)
A Christian witness is one, who by faith and example, shares faith in Jesus Christ with others.

Worship (page 27)
Worship is praise and thanks to God in word, action, and signs.

Yahweh (page 76)
God's name as it was given to Moses. It means "I am who am."

Our Catholic Identity

Thy Kingdom Come

When Jesus founded the Church, he told Saint Peter, "I will give you the keys to the kingdom of heaven" (Matthew 16:19). Under the leadership of Peter and his successors, the Church would continue to proclaim the good news of God's kingdom in every age until the end of the world.

At the end of the world, Jesus will come again. Then the last judgement will take place. Jesus will judge us according to the way we have lived our lives as his followers.

Those who have died in God's grace and friendship will be rewarded with heaven. Those who have freely chosen to reject God will be separated from him for all eternity. This separation is called hell.

Those who are not yet ready for heaven but who died in God's grace and friendship must experience a period of purification to prepare them for heaven. This is called purgatory. God does not wish anyone to be separated from him. We ask God to help us choose a life that will lead us to heaven.

Learn by heart **Faith Summary**

- Jesus preached the good news of the kingdom of God.

- The kingdom of God is the saving power of God's life and love in the world.

- We build up the kingdom of God by working for love, justice, and peace in our world.

1

The Cardinal Virtues

We know that the theological virtues are gifts from God. There are other virtues, however, that we can develop in ourselves with the help of God's grace. These are called *human virtues*. These virtues are habits that grow each and every time we try to do what is good.

In Catholic teaching, four of these virtues are very important, and for this reason they are called the *cardinal virtues*. They are prudence, justice, fortitude, and temperance.

The virtue of *prudence* gives us correct knowledge about the things we should do and the things that we should avoid. Prudence leads us to take the good advice of others.

The virtue of *justice* helps us to give all people what is due to them. A just person treats everyone fairly and respects the rights of everyone as God wants.

The virtue of *fortitude* helps us to conquer our fears and to be strong in living our faith. Fortitude also helps us to overcome difficulties in our lives.

The virtue of *temperance* helps to have discipline in our lives—in what we eat, in what we drink, and in what we do. It is important to eat, for example, but too much food or too little food can make us sick. A disciple of Jesus can enjoy the good things of life, but with the gentle control of temperance.

PRUDENCE

Pray every day that the Holy Spirit will guide you in living the four cardinal virtues.

Learn by heart Faith Summary

- Faith enables us to believe and trust in God.

- Hope enables us to have full confidence in God, no matter what happens.

- Love enables us to love God, ourselves, and our neighbors.

2

Can Laws Change?

The Ten Commandments are laws that can never be changed. This is because they are God's laws, and God wants us to obey them all our lives.

There are some laws, however, that do change. We call these *human laws*. Human laws can be made by the government or by the Church. They are made to help people for a certain time in history.

People in your family may remember when Catholics who wanted to receive Holy Communion had to fast from food and liquid—including water—from midnight. But as parish Mass schedules and people's working schedules changed, the Church decided to change the law. Now we are required to fast for only one hour before receiving Communion.

This change was made to encourage Catholics to receive Holy Communion more frequently.

All laws are important. The Church guides us in understanding which laws are God's laws and which laws are human laws. Take time to ask your grandparents or other adults about Church laws that have changed during their lifetime.

Learn by heart · Faith Summary

- God gave Moses the Ten Commandments to give to the people.

- The Ten Commandments help us to live with true freedom as God's people.

- The Ten Commandments help us to live the Law of Love, which Jesus taught.

3

Fifth Station: Simon helps Jesus carry His cross.

Stations of the Cross

Jesus Christ is the Savior of the world. Jesus is our Redeemer and Liberator. He saved, or freed, us from our sins. Jesus did this through his life, his death on the cross, and his resurrection.

For centuries, people have traveled to the Holy Land to follow in the footsteps of Jesus as he carried the cross to Calvary. Not everyone was able to make this journey, however. That is why Catholics began the custom of remembering Jesus' suffering and death by praying the stations of the cross.

The stations of the cross are fourteen pictures or carvings placed inside a parish church. These stations tell the story of Jesus as he traveled on his way to Calvary. They are called stations because the fourteen pictures are places where people stop and stand to remember and pray about the sufferings of Christ.

Praying the Stations

When we pray the stations, we begin with Pilate condemning Jesus to death, and we end with Jesus' burial in the tomb. Why not make a visit to your parish church to pray the stations of the cross? Stop at each station. Look at what is happening in each. Put yourself in the picture with Jesus. Then pray this prayer:

† We adore you, O Christ, and we praise you, because by your holy cross you have redeemed the world.

Learn by heart **Faith Summary**

- We can sin in thought, word, or action.

- Very serious sins are called mortal sins; less serious sins are called venial sins.

- A sin is mortal when what we do is very seriously wrong; we know that it is very wrong and that God forbids it; we freely choose to do it.

4

Statues and Crucifixes

Some people wonder why Catholics have statues and crucifixes in their homes and churches. They think that having crucifixes and statues is against the first commandment—that Catholics are adoring images. But Catholics do not worship images. We use them only to turn our minds and hearts to God in prayer. We worship God alone.

Catholics use the crucifix to remind us of Jesus and all that he did for us. We use statues of the Blessed Virgin Mary and the other saints to remind us of their holy lives and to ask them to pray for us.

Many Catholic families place a crucifix in a bedroom or another room of the house. Another Catholic custom is to have a statue of the Blessed Virgin Mary or one of the saints, or some other kind of religious art, in our homes. Good religious art helps us to pray and reminds us to live as Jesus' disciples.

What religious art would you like to choose? What will it help you to remember?

Learn by heart Faith Summary

- The first commandment is "I, the LORD, am your God, who brought you out of . . . that place of slavery. You shall not have other gods besides me."

- Jesus taught us to put God first in our lives.

- When we live the first commandment, we live in true freedom.

5

Time for God

The Church reminds us that it is important to be on time for Mass. When we deliberately choose to arrive late for the celebration of the Eucharist, we show disrespect for the assembly and for God.

It is a good practice to arrive a few minutes early for Mass. It gives us time to pray quietly and think about the tremendous things that are about to happen in the celebration of the Eucharist. It is a good time to kneel and pray to Jesus, who is present in the Blessed Sacrament. The lighted sanctuary lamp reminds us that the Blessed Sacrament is in the tabernacle.

Just as we should arrive early, we must not leave Mass before the celebration is completed. Each part of the Mass is important. Unless we have a good excuse, we should plan on being at the entire celebration so that we may worship God fully with our community.

Learn by heart **Faith Summary**

- The third commandment is "Remember to keep holy the sabbath day."

- Christians celebrate their sabbath on Sunday. We remember that Jesus rose from the dead on Easter Sunday.

- Catholics must take part in the Mass on Sunday or on Saturday evening and on all holy days of obligation.

The Presentation of the Lord

The Gospel of Saint Luke tells a wonderful story about the Holy Family. Soon after Jesus was born, Joseph and Mary took him to the Temple in the city of Jerusalem. They did this to follow the Jewish law that the firstborn male child was to be presented, or dedicated, to God.

Each year on February 2, Catholics celebrate the feast of the Presentation of the Lord. On this day we remember the presentation of Jesus in the Temple. We hear the words of Luke's Gospel reminding us that Jesus is the Light of the World. For that reason, this is also the day that the Church chooses to bless candles that will be used for worship all during the year.

The Blessing of Candles

As the ceremony of blessing candles begins, people may gather outside the parish church with unlighted candles. While the candles are being lighted, the people sing a hymn in praise of Christ our Light. Then the priest blesses the candles and asks God to make them holy. He prays that we who carry them to praise God will "walk in the path of goodness and come to the light that shines for ever."

The next time you see lighted candles in church, remember the story of the Holy Family and the feast of the Presentation of the Lord. Pray that you, too, will walk in the path of goodness.

Learn by heart **Faith Summary**

- The fourth commandment is "Honor your father and your mother."

- Jesus showed us how to keep the fourth commandment.

- The fourth commandment teaches us to honor and obey all who take care of us.

Caring for Life

Did you know that the Catholic Church runs many hospitals and other places that care for the sick and the aged? The Church has always carried on Jesus' ministry of promoting life and helping people in pain.

Many religious communities are involved in this kind of healing ministry. For example, the Sisters of Mercy and the Sisters of Charity have built and run many large hospitals in the United States. The Alexian Brothers have a similar ministry.

Through an organization called Catholic Charities, the dioceses of the United States support homes for the elderly and disabled. In our own time, many men, women, and children are suffering from AIDS. The Church is deeply concerned for them and shows Jesus' love by providing places for them to live and to receive treatment, as well as spiritual care and love.

Catholic hospitals and health care facilities are places of love and life. They are always looking for members of the Church to volunteer time in support of their ministry and the people for whom they care. Perhaps one day you can join in their wonderful ministry, too.

Pray together:
✝ O God, be with all those who are sick or elderly. Comfort them with your great love. Amen.

Learn by heart **Faith Summary**

- The fifth commandment is "You shall not kill." It teaches us that all human life is sacred.

- All people have an equal right to life and to be treated with justice.

- We choose life when we care for all people and the world around us.

The Banns of Marriage

The Catholic Church teaches that marriage is a sacrament between a baptized man and woman. This means that it is a way of holiness for men and women and a gift of God. It also means that marriage is a gift to the whole Church. This is why marriage is celebrated in public with witnesses, not in private.

Catholics who want to be married meet with their parish priest. He helps them to prepare to celebrate the sacrament. He also may publish what is known as the *banns of marriage.*

The word *banns* means the public announcement of a future marriage. Usually the announcement of a couple's marriage is published in the parish bulletin or newspaper. Sometimes their names are read out at Mass. In this way, the whole Church family knows when its members are about to be married. The banns are normally published or announced for three weeks before the wedding ceremony.

Find out if and how the banns of marriage are posted in your parish. When you see or hear the banns, pray that the couples being married will be faithful marriage partners for their entire lives.

Banns of Marriage

I Anna Ortiz and Jorge Santiago

II Tai Chun and Lu Kwan

III Virginia Martin and Thomas Nadramia

Learn by heart **Faith Summary**

- The sixth commandment is "You shall not commit adultery." The ninth commandment is "You shall not covet your neighbor's wife."

- We do not do anything to our own body or to another person's body that is disrespectful in thought or word or action.

- To be faithful means to be loyal and true to someone.

Witnesses to the Truth

All during the year, Catholics celebrate the memory of men and women who gave up their lives for the truth of the Christian faith. We call these brave and courageous people martyrs. The word martyr means "witness," and a witness is someone who tells the truth either in word or in action.

When the Church began, there were many people who did not like or understand the disciples of Jesus Christ. Often the early Christians were persecuted and even put to death for their faith. When this happened, the Church remembered the words of Jesus from the Beatitudes:
"Blessed are they who are persecuted . . .
　for theirs is the kingdom of heaven."
(Matthew 5:10).

The stories of the martyrs are stories of great faith and courage. You may wish to learn more about the stories of the apostles and first disciples, many of whom were martyred for their faith in Jesus Christ. You can also read about other early martyrs such as Saint Lucy, Saint Cecilia, and Saint Agnes.

Martyrs are not just people from the past, however. Christians are still persecuted for their faith today. You may want to read more about the lives of modern martyrs such as Archbishop Oscar Romero and the four courageous women who died in the country of El Salvador doing missionary work.

Miguel Pro, SJ, Mexican Jesuit, executed for the faith, 1927.

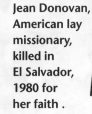

Jean Donovan, American lay missionary, killed in El Salvador, 1980 for her faith.

Learn by heart Faith Summary

- The eighth commandment is "You shall not bear false witness against your neighbor."

- This commandment teaches us that it is wrong to lie, to tell someone's secrets, or to gossip.

- A person who has the courage to tell and live the truth is a true disciple of Jesus Christ.

Symbols for the Holy Spirit

The symbol for the Holy Spirit that is best known to most Catholics is the *dove*. Very often in our parish churches we see this symbol in stained-glass windows or in other works of art. The symbol reminds us of the gospel story of Jesus' baptism by John the Baptist in the Jordan River: Jesus saw the Spirit of God decending like a dove and coming upon him.

The dove is not the only symbol we use to remind us of the Holy Spirit, however. Another symbol is *fire* or a *flame*. When the Holy Spirit first came upon the disciples of Jesus after his resurrection, the Spirit was said to have come like small flames of fire (Based on Acts 2:3).

Sometimes the symbols of *cloud* and *light* are used to help us remember the Holy Spirit, too. Once when Jesus was with his apostles Peter, James, and John high on a mountaintop, he was transfigured, or changed, in a brilliant light before their eyes. A cloud came over them, and they heard God say that Jesus was God's own Son. You can read all about it in Luke 9:28–35.

The dove, fire, cloud, and light are just a few symbols for the Holy Spirit. Think for a moment. What beautiful symbol can you make to help remind yourself and others of God the Holy Spirit?

Learn by heart Faith Summary

- God the Holy Spirit fills each of us with special gifts.

- The gifts of the Holy Spirit are wisdom, understanding, right judgment, courage, knowledge, reverence, and wonder and awe.

- When we pray for guidance, God the Holy Spirit will help us to make the right choices.

11

Easter Duty

It is a law of the Church that we receive Holy Communion at least once a year between the First Sunday of Lent and Trinity Sunday. The Church made this law for a special reason.

A long time ago, some Catholics began to think that they should not receive Holy Communion frequently. They thought they were not worthy to receive our Lord Jesus Christ himself each week. They were forgetting why Jesus gave us the gift of himself in Holy Communion—to nourish us often and to strengthen us in living as his disciples.

That is why the Church wisely made the law to receive Holy Communion at least once during the seasons of Lent and Easter. The practice of receiving Communion during this time became known as "making our Easter duty."

We should not think of receiving Communion only as a duty, however. It is a great privilege and joy for us to receive Jesus. Even though we are never fully worthy of this great honor, Jesus wants us to receive him often in Holy Communion. He comes to us as our Bread of Life.

Use these words from the Mass to prepare yourself for Holy Communion:

Lord, I am not worthy to receive you, but only say the word and I shall be healed.

Learn by heart Faith Summary

- The Holy Spirit guides the whole Church in continuing Jesus' mission.
- Each baptized person has something special to do to carry on Jesus' mission.
- The laws of the Church help us to live as good Catholics.

The Sacred Heart of Jesus

The heart has always been a symbol of love. For Catholics, the heart of Jesus is a symbol of his great love for us. Because Jesus is both divine and human, he loves us as no one else can.

Each year soon after Pentecost, we celebrate the feast of the Sacred Heart of Jesus. Catholics do this to celebrate the love and forgiveness of God that comes to us in Jesus Christ our Savior.

Catholics often pray a litany in honor of the Sacred Heart of Jesus. A litany is a prayer in which we call repeatedly upon Jesus or Mary or the saints, using special titles or names. After each title or name, the community makes a response.

Here are two of the titles we use in the litany of the Sacred Heart. The response to each is "have mercy on us."

Heart of Jesus,
patient and full of mercy,
have mercy on us.

Heart of Jesus,
delight of all the saints,
have mercy on us.

At the end of the litany of the Sacred Heart, we pray together:

Jesus, gentle and humble of heart,
Touch our hearts and make
them like your own.

Try to find the complete litany of the Sacred Heart and pray it together.

Learn by heart Faith Summary

- Our conscience helps us to decide what is right or wrong.

- With the help of the Holy Spirit, we examine our conscience by asking ourselves how well we have lived God's law.

- We examine our conscience before celebrating the sacrament of Reconciliation.

13

Confessing Our Sins

When Catholics go to confession, they usually celebrate the sacrament either in a reconciliation room or a confessional box. These are the usual places for the celebration of the sacrament. But do you know that a priest can hear confessions at any time and in any place?

When Catholics are sick and unable to go to the church, the priest will go to them. He can hear their confession in their homes or at the hospital. A priest is always happy to visit the sick and celebrate the sacrament of Reconciliation, as well as the sacrament of Anointing of the Sick with them.

Whether he is at home or traveling, a priest may be called upon to hear confessions in an emergency. For example, a priest may give absolution at the scene of an accident. Some priests who work as military chaplains even celebrate this sacrament on battlefields or aboard warships.

The Church wants the grace of the sacrament of Reconciliation to be available to us at all times. All of us are called to a deep appreciation of this sacrament and to celebrate it regularly.

Learn by heart **Faith Summary**

- We celebrate God's mercy and forgiveness in the sacrament of Reconciliation.

- We can take part in the sacrament of Reconciliation alone with the priest or with the community and the priest.

- Jesus asks us to be reconcilers in our family, neighborhood, school, and world.

14

The Feast of Corpus Christi

Each year on the second Sunday after Pentecost, the Church celebrates the feast of the Body and Blood of Christ. Catholics also call this day the feast of Corpus Christi. The words *Corpus Christi* are Latin for "the Body of Christ."

Corpus Christi is a wonderful day on which Catholics all around the world remember and celebrate the real presence of Christ in the Eucharist. On this day, we take the time to show special love and reverence for the Eucharist, our Bread of Life.

Very often a parish community will have a procession with the Blessed Sacrament. The whole parish gathers behind the priest or deacon, who carries the Blessed Sacrament in a special container in which the Host can be seen. The container is called the *monstrance.* If the weather is good, the procession might even go outside the church to the surrounding neighborhood.

In some countries, everyone joins in the procession, especially in small towns and villages. Sometimes the procession will start at the parish church, move through the very center of the town, and return to the Church again.

Invite your family or friends to make a visit with you to the Blessed Sacrament this week. Spend a few moments in prayer with Jesus.

Learn by heart **Faith Summary**

- The Mass is made up of the Liturgy of the Word and the Liturgy of the Eucharist.

- We listen to readings from the Bible during the Liturgy of the Word.

- During the Liturgy of the Eucharist the bread and wine become the Body and Blood of Christ.

15

INDEX

**Bold-faced pages indicate chapters

†*Italics* refer to definitions

*Bold-faced pages indicate chapters

†*Italics* refer to definitions

Answers for Reviews

Lesson 1 (pg. 18): **1.** c **2.** b **3.** c **4.** c
Lesson 2 (pg. 24): **1.** b **2.** a **3.** c **4.** b
Lesson 3 (pg. 30): **1.** b **2.** a **3.** b **4.** c
Lesson 4 (pg. 36): **1.** the humble **2.** God **3.** peacemakers **4.** the pure of heart
Lesson 5 (pg. 42): **1.** Corporal **2.** Feed the hungry **3.** Spiritual **4.** Forgive those who hurt us
Lesson 6 (pg. 48): **1.** T **2.** F **3.** T **4.** T
Lesson 7 (pg. 54): **1.** Mass **2.** Body, Blood **3.** Word **4.** bread, wine
Unit 1 (pg. 56): **1.** c **2.** b **3.** c **4.** b
Lesson 8 (pg. 62): **1.** c **2.** c **3.** b **4.** b
Lesson 9 (pg. 68): **1.** c **2.** a **3.** a **4.** c
Lesson 10 (pg. 74): 4, 3, 1, 2
Lesson 11 (pg. 80): **1.** to honor God's name **2.** calling on God to be our witness **3.** Yahweh **4.** because cursing is wishing evil on someone

Lesson 12 (pg. 86): **1.** staying in bed all day **2.** work harder **3.** the first Christmas **4.** feast days
Lesson 13 (pg. 92): 4, 3, 1, 2
Lesson 14 (pg. 98): 4, 1, 2, 3
Summary 1 (pg. 101): **1.** b **2.** c **3.** b **4.** a **5.** c **6.** Ten Commandments **7.** sin **8.** first **9.** Father **10.** Sunday
Lesson 15 (pg. 108): **1.** Honor **2.** Mary, Joseph **3.** parents **4.** respect
Lesson 16 (pg. 114): **1.** c **2.** a **3.** c **4.** c
Lesson 17 (pg. 120): **1.** faithfully **2.** wife or husband **3.** adultery **4.** respect
Lesson 18 (pg. 126): **1.** not to steal **2.** be greedy **3.** taking without permission **4.** stealing someone's answers
Lesson 19 (pg. 132): **1.** spread gossip about **2.** never **3.** truthful **4.** doing something harmful
Lesson 20 (pg. 138): **1.** F **2.** F **3.** T **4.** T

Lesson 21 (pg. 144): **1.** The Easter Triduum **2.** Jesus suffered, carried the cross, and died on the cross. **3.** The gift of the Eucharist **4.** Alleluia
Unit 3 (pg. 146): **1.** d **2.** a **3.** b **4.** c
Lesson 22 (pg. 152): **1.** c **2.** c **3.** c **4.** b
Lesson 23 (pg. 158): 3, 1, 4, 2
Lesson 24 (pg. 164): **1.** conscience **2.** Law of Love **3.** practicing **4.** Holy Spirit
Lesson 25 (pg. 170): **1.** forgiven **2.** God **3.** alone, others **4.** Reconciliation
Lesson 26 (pg. 176): **1.** c **2.** c **3.** c **4.** b
Lesson 27 (pg. 182): 3, 4, 1, 2
Lesson 28 (pg. 188): **1.** rosary **2.** visitation **3.** decade **4.** assumption
Summary 2 (pg. 191–192): **1.** c **2.** a **3.** d **4.** c **5.** b **6.** Reconciliation **7.** Bible **8.** consecrated **9.** Holy Spirit **10.** pope **11.** 5 **12.** 6 or 9 **13.** 4 **14.** 7 or 10 **15.** 8

Acknowledgments

Grateful acknowledgment is due the following for their work on the *Coming to Faith* Program:
Maureen Gallo, Editor
Tresse De Lorenzo, Manager: Production/Art
Joe Svadlenka, Art Director
Dolores Keller, Design Manager
Matt Straub, Designer

Scripture selections are taken from the *New American Bible*, copyright © 1991, 1986, 1970 by the Confraternity of Christian Doctrine, Washington, D.C. and are used with permission. All rights reserved.

Excerpts from the English translation of *Rite of Baptism for Children* © 1969, International Committee on English in the Liturgy, Inc. (ICEL); excerpts from the English translation of *The Roman Missal* © 1973, ICEL; excerpts from the English translation of *Rite of Penance* © 1974, ICEL. All rights reserved. English translation of the Lord's Prayer, Gloria Patri, and the Apostles' Creed by the International Consultation on English Texts.

Photo Research

Jim Saylor

Cover Photos

Myrleen Cate

Photo Credits

Diane J. Ali: 22 *center right*, 125, 217.
Dennis Barnes: 153 *bottom left*, 166, 227.
Myrleen Cate: 8 *right*, 9, 22 *center left*, 26/27, 32, 33, 40, 44, 45, 60, 64, 65, 72, 76 *left*, 77 *insets*, 104, 105, 106, 110 *left*, 111, 117, 118, 119, 122 *top*, 123, 124, 135, 150, 153 *top*, 162, 167, 168, 173 *insets*, 174, 183, 193, 194, 197, 198, 207, 215, 225.
Catholic News Service: 221, 223.
CROSIERS/ Gene Plaisted, OSC: 134, 172/173, 214, 216, 218, 219, 220.
Giraudon/ Art Resource, NY: 50.
LIAISON International/ Jean Michel Turpin: 153 *bottom right*.

National Museum of Auschwitz-Birkenau, Oswiecim, Poland, courtesy of the United States Holocaust Memorial Museum: 177 *top*.
Photo Edit/ James Shaffer: 13 *right*; Bill Aron: 82 *bottom*.
Francisco J. Rangel: 186.
H. Armstrong Roberts: 8/9 *background*, 13 *left*, 22 *top*, 22 *bottom*, 142, 160/161.
Frances M. Roberts: 122 *bottom*.
Michael Schimpf: 226.
James Shaffer: 228.
Nancy Sheehan: 8 *left*, 76 *right*, 82 *top*.
Tate Gallery, London/ Art Resource, NY: 184.
Tony Stone Images/ Tony Craddock: 14/15 *background*; Brian Bailey: 69; Steve Leonard: 76/77; Andy Cox: 110 *right*; Peter Pearson: 116; Stephen Studd: 177 *bottom*.

Illustrators

Blaine Martin: Cover, Digital Imaging
Wendy Pierson: Cover, Logo Rendering

Gil Ashby: 35
David Barnett: 20–21, 81, 88–89
Andrea Barrett: 52
Shirley Beckes: 91
Teresa Berasi: 134–135
Alex Bloch: 178–179
Jean Bowler: 148–149
Amy Bryant: 122–123, 124
Kevin Butler: 26–27, 76, 77, 125, 136, 137, 150, 153, 157, 160–161, 173
Cameron Clement: 72, 73
Gwen Connelly: 143
Don Dyen: 109
Barbara Epstein Eagle: 106, 107
Bill Farnsworth: 25
Joseph Forte: 58–59
Kristen Goeters: 49, 159
Grace Goldberg: 162
Adam Gordon: 60, 119
Susan Greenstein: 61
Pat DeWitt Grush: 87

Marika Hahn: 133
Brad Hamann: 63, 64–65, 169
John Haysom: 171
Monica Higgins: 28, 34
Rex Irvine: 14
Jeff Jones: 78, 79
Helen Kunze: 51
Victoria Lisi: 115
Lyn Martin: 12, 13, 46, 47
Bert Mayse: 130, 131
Darlene Olivia McElroy: 32–33, 104–105, 163
Peg McGovern: 75
David Scott Meier: 82, 83
Deborah Haley Melmon: 53, 187
Lucy Montgomery: 7
Cindy Patrick: 168
Bob Pepper: 127, 165
Julie Peterson: 40, 41
Wendy Pierson: 151, 186
Deborah Pinkney: 10, 96, 97
Fernando Rangel: 26–27, 37, 38–39
Alan Reingold: 19, 31, 70–71
Dorothy Reinhardt: 23, 174, 175
Lainé Roundy: 90
Margaret Sanfilippo: 103, 178–179
Sally Schaedler: 121, 147, 183
Evan Schwarze: 180, 181
David Seibert: 94–95
Scott Snow: 128, 129
Mark Sparacio: 166–167
Tom Sperling: 43, 93
Jim Starr: 44–45, 154, 155
Matt Straub: 57, 113
Mary Thelan: 84
Winson Trang: 66, 67, 112
Gregg Valley: 11, 29, 85, 116–117, 118, 156
Lehner & Whyte: 139, 140–141
Dean Wilhite: 16, 17
Mary O'Keefe Young: 184–185